CW00496031

IPSWICH TO SAXMUNDHAM

Richard Adderson and
Graham Kenworthy
Series editor Vic Mitchell

MP Middleton Press

Cover picture: "Sandringham" class 4-6-0 no. 61670 ***City of London*** *was recorded at Woodbridge on 10th October 1956 with the 7.30am from Yarmouth South Town. It was due at Liverpool Street at 10.31. (R.C.Riley)*

First Published February 2000

ISBN 1 901706 41 9

© Middleton Press, 2000

Design Deborah Esher

Published by
Middleton Press
Easebourne Lane
Midhurst, West Sussex
GU29 9AZ
Tel: 01730 813169
Fax: 01730 812601

Printed & bound by Biddles Ltd,
Guildford and Kings Lynn

CONTENTS

INDEX

ACKNOWLEDGEMENTS

In addition to the photographers acknowledged in the photographic credits, we are most grateful to the following people for their assistance in the compilation of this book: J.Day, C.Fisher, R.Kingstone, A.Sibley and M.Storey-Smith.

Readers of this book may be interested in the following society;
Great Eastern Railway Society
J.R.Tant, Membership Secretary
9 Clare Road, Leytonstone
London E11 1JU

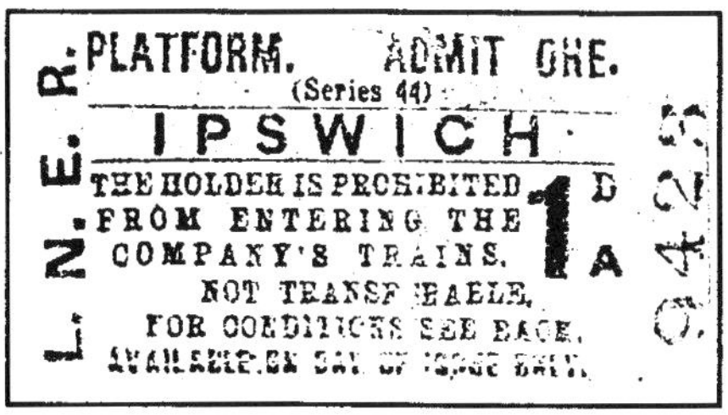

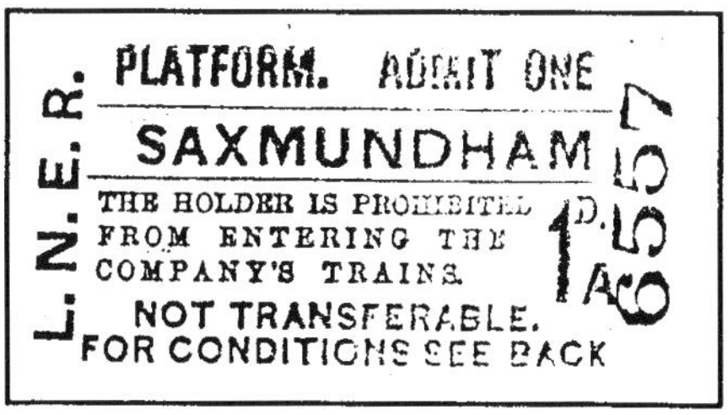

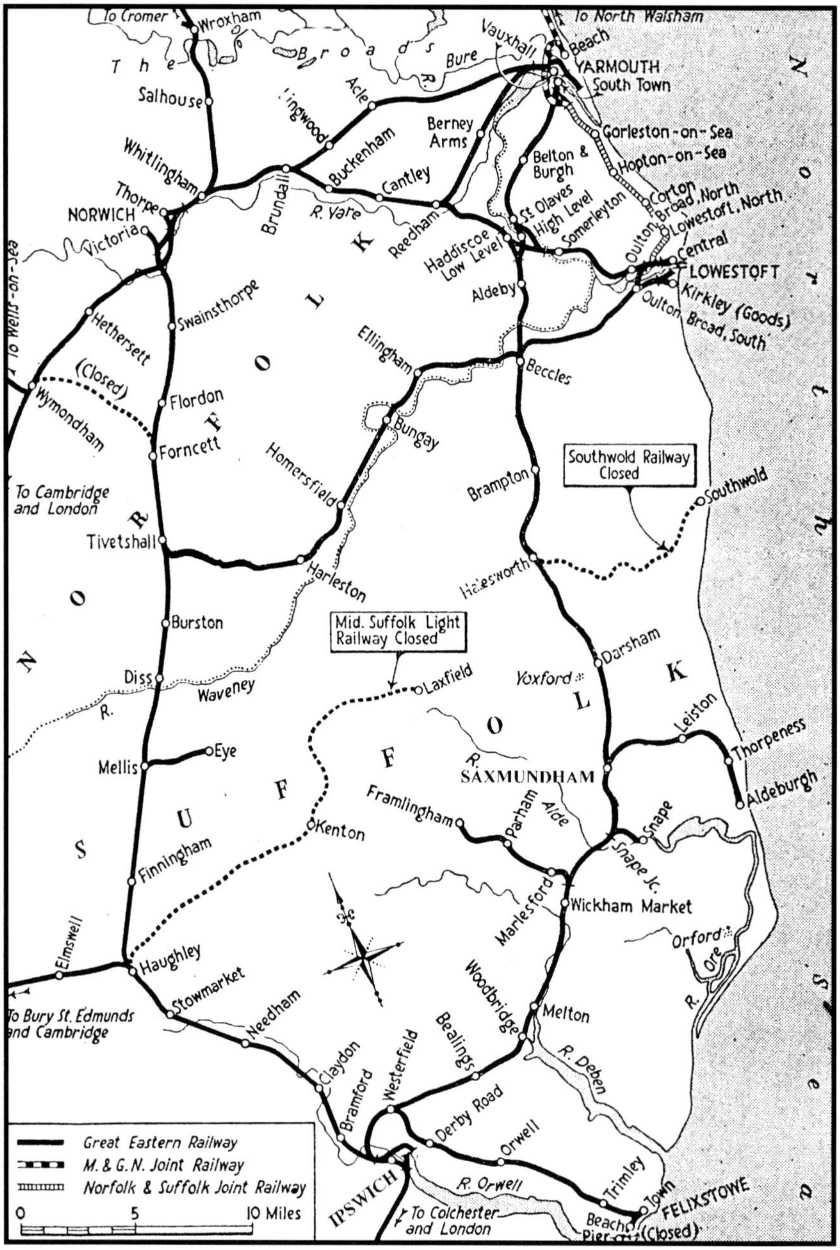

Railways of the area in 1954. The pre-1923 ownerships are shown, but not all the stations on the minor lines are marked. The other maps in this volume are to the scale of 1 ins to 25 miles. (Railway Magazine)

GEOGRAPHICAL SETTING

The line is essentially a coastal one, following the gentle curve of the Suffolk coast. At East Suffolk Junction, Ipswich, it is approximately twelve miles from the coast as the crow flies, while at Saxmundham it is barely six miles from the sea. The 21 mile route passes through pleasantly undulating countryside, apart from the initial section through the north-west suburbs of Ipswich and the run through the largely residential communities of Woodbridge and Melton, On the portion of the line covered in this volume, there have been a total of three branches, two heading towards the coast, and one inland. The inland branch, to Framlingham, is included with the main line; those branches following an easterly or south-easterly route will be the subject of a later volume.

The railway was built to follow the contours, so keeping major earthworks and structures to a minimum. Because of this, and the fact that the route runs broadly parallel to the coast, its gradient profile is a series of peaks and troughs, as the line climbs out of, and descends into, successive river valleys, each of which is virtually at sea level.

The line starts at the 69½ mile post from Liverpool Street, in the valley of the Gipping, the river on which Ipswich stands. There is then a sharp climb of just over two miles to a summit at Westerfield, before a long, rather gentler, descent, following the River Fynn, a tributary of the Deben, to the west bank of the latter at Woodbridge, at the 79 mile post. After skirting the river and then crossing it three times in 4½ miles on mainly rising gradients, the line climbs steeply to another summit at Wickham Market station.

From Wickham Market, the route drops almost as steeply, and then follows the River Ore downstream from Wickham Market Junction, to the River Alde, which it crosses at about 87½ miles. From here the line generally climbs past the site of Snape Junction towards Saxmundham, but the final approach is down at 1 in 98 to the 91 mile post.

The Framlingham branch started at Wickham Market Junction, adjacent to Blackstock level crossing; from this point it descended briefly before taking a north-westerly direction to follow the River Ore upstream all the way to Framlingham, 91 miles from London, on mostly rising gradients.

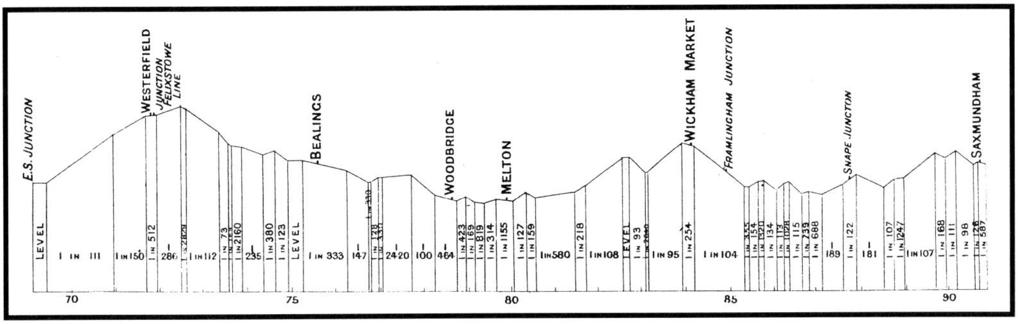

Gradient Diagram with the mileage shown from London.

HISTORICAL BACKGROUND

The southern section of the line as finally constructed and opened had its earliest origins in the Ipswich & Bury Railway (Woodbridge Extension) Act of 1847, although construction was not carried out at this early date and the powers lapsed. A number of schemes in the north-east of the county had also been proposed in the Railway Mania years of the late 1840s, but all had failed.

However, various forces, not least that of Samuel Morton Peto, in the area around Beccles and Halesworth decided that a rather simpler scheme might succeed. This new approach led to the successful promotion of a line heading north into Norfolk, the Halesworth, Beccles & Haddiscoe Railway. The Act was passed in 1851, and the line opened to passengers in December 1854.

This success of 1851 led to renewed efforts to complete the route southwards from Halesworth towards Ipswich. The objective was achieved in two stages, both in 1854; an Act authorising the section from Halesworth to Woodbridge (and the change of name to the East Suffolk Railway) and renewed powers granted to the Eastern Union Railway under the Ipswich & Bury Act of 1847 referred to above. (The EUR and I&BR had amalgamated in 1847). The 1854 East Suffolk Act also authorised the branches to Leiston, Snape and Framlingham.

There were further developments and complications at the northern end of the line which will be dealt with in a later volume. It is sufficient to say here that the East Suffolk Railway opened throughout on 1st June 1859. This opening involved the double track main line from Ipswich East Suffolk Junction to Yarmouth South Town, together with the single line branches to Framlingham, Snape, Leiston and Lowestoft. All stations covered in this volume with the exception of Hacheston Halt were opened with the lines.

In the meantime, various leases and mergers had taken place, and these led ultimately to the formation of the Great Eastern Railway by Act of Parliament on 7th August 1862, by amalgamation of the Eastern Counties, the Eastern Union, the Norfolk, the East Suffolk and the East Anglian Railways.

The only other later development which need concern us here was the opening of the branch from Westerfield to Felixstowe which was privately promoted and opened in 1877; this, too, will be covered in a later volume.

The Great Eastern Railway passed into the ownership of the London & North Eastern Railway on 1st January 1923, the lines became part of the Eastern Region of British Railways upon Nationalisation on 1st January 1948. During the 86 year period of GER and LNER ownership there were few major developments, apart from the gradual introduction of interlocking to the signalling system.

In the early years of State ownership a critical appraisal was made of lightly used passenger services, resulting in a number of closures in the early 1950s. Amongst the casualties was the branch service from Wickham Market to Framlingham which was withdrawn on 3rd November 1952, although the line still saw some special passenger services (mainly for the pupils of Framlingham College), while a freight service continued until 19th April 1965.

The infamous Beeching Report of March 1963 proposed the closure to passengers of the whole of the East Suffolk line. In the event the through route was reprieved by the Minister of Transport in 1966, although by then all stations except Melton had been closed to freight.

Revised services planned in connection with conductor-guard working were introduced on schedule on 11th November 1966, but the actual on-train issuing of tickets was delayed until 6th March 1967, on which date all stations became unstaffed halts.

In 1984 preparatory work began on rationalisation of the route and the automation of all level crossings, culminating in the introduction of Radio Electronic Tokenless Block (RETB) on 16th February 1986. The line was singled between Woodbridge and Saxmundham (and further north between Halesworth and Oulton Broad North Junction) and conventional signalling abolished, all train movements being controlled and monitored from the adapted signalbox at Saxmundham.

Since introduction of RETB working northwards from Westerfield, regular freight traffic has been confined to the southern end of the line, branching off at Saxmundham to serve Sizewell siding and its associated nuclear power station. This is, of course, in addition to the large volume of container traffic between East Suffolk Junction and Westerfield en route to and from Felixstowe.

Following Privatisation the remaining passenger services are operated by Anglia Railways, while freight services to Sizewell and Felixstowe are in the hands of DRS and Freightliner respectively.

PASSENGER SERVICES

Because the East Suffolk Line and its branches served a number of holiday resorts from Felixstowe at the south end to Yarmouth at the northern terminus, it inevitably saw its most intensive use on Summer Saturdays during July and August. However, this book is concerned with the wider picture and, therefore, this section concentrates on the "bread-and-butter", year-round situation. With the exception of the timetable for August 1859, which is included to show the earliest services on the line, all other examples quoted are from winter period timetables and refer to trains which ran on weekdays. Suffice to say that, as far as the Summer Saturday service was concerned, British Railways still provided, as late as 1965 (two years after the Beeching Report), ten through trains (plus another three involving a change at Ipswich) from Liverpool Street to Lowestoft and Yarmouth South Town via the East Suffolk Line between 07.00 and 13.30. In addition, two other trains provided a link from London to Aldeburgh with just one change at Ipswich.

The first East Suffolk Railway timetable published in the Ipswich Advertiser, that for August 1859, showed five up trains from Saxmundham to Ipswich, all originating from Yarmouth. The first, at 6.55 am, and the last, at 7.18 pm, both designated "Parliamentary", called at all stations, while the 11.44 am and the 4.41 pm did not stop at Bealings or Westerfield. The other train, the 7.35 am, identified as "Express", ran non-stop to Ipswich, having left Yarmouth 65 minutes later than the morning "Parliamentary", but arriving at Ipswich only 5 minutes behind.

The down service from Ipswich was similar but with three trains, the 6.50 am, the 12 mid-day and the 6.50 pm calling at all stations, with only the 2.35 pm not stopping at Westerfield and Bealings. The down "Express" left at 6.40 pm, running non-stop to Saxmundham.

By the March 1882 Great Eastern timetable the number of up trains had only increased to six but the times had altered considerably. Three of the trains called at all stations between Saxmundham and Ipswich, while a fourth only failed to call at Westerfield. There were two equivalents of the earlier "Express", leaving at 9.29 am and 3.27 pm calling only at Wickham Market and Woodbridge, although the former was allowed to stop at Melton and Bealings to pick up London passengers only.

In contrast, the down service consisted of seven trains, four of which called at all stations. The 11.57 am and 4.38 pm from Ipswich did not stop at Westerfield, Bealings and Melton while the 5.18 pm made only one intermediate stop, at Woodbridge.

By this time Westerfield had gained slightly with the opening of the Felixstowe Branch in 1877, two of the branch trains stopping in each direction.

There had been a further increase of one service in each direction by the April 1910 timetable. There were three up trains which called at all stations and three more which only omitted a stop at Westerfield; the morning express now left Saxmundham at 9.23 am and ran non-stop to Ipswich, all other stations having been served by the 8.51 am departure. The up "East Anglian" Dining Car Train, the 6.5 pm from Yarmouth to Liverpool Street did not call at any stations between Halesworth and Ipswich.

The down service of eight trains had a slightly different pattern with two "all stations", three "all stations except Westerfield" and one "all stations except Melton". The remaining two stopped only at Woodbridge and Wickham Market.

In December 1938 six of the 1910 up trains still ran in virtually the same paths. Four additional trains, three of them "all stations", and one calling only at Wickham Market, had been added, while the former "East Anglian" now ran later and stopped at Saxmundham from where it was non-stop to Ipswich, giving Saxmundham a total of eleven daily trains to the county town.

The down service showed even more similarity with that of 1910, all trains from that year still following identifiable timings, but with different stopping patterns. However, there were four additional trains, two of which were non-stop between Ipswich and Saxmundham. The latter also benefitted from the inclusion of a stop in the late afternoon express, which in 1910 ran non-stop to Beccles. These alterations gave Saxmundham a total of thirteen down services daily.

The Winter 1951/2 timetable showed a similar level of service in both directions but with less trains stopping at intermediate stations, Bealings and Melton being the biggest casualties.

Following the closure of Bealings and Melton and dieselisation, the January 1961 Bradshaw showed a remarkable increase in the number of trains with no less than 20 trains running each day between Ipswich and Saxmundham and 23 in the opposite direction. Of those in the down direction, only six stopped at Westerfield and five stopped only at Woodbridge; the pattern in the up direction being broadly similar.

Diversion of London to Yarmouth through services via Norwich, the effects of the Beeching Report and the introduction of Paytrain services reversed this generous situation dramatically, so that by the Winter of 1969/70 as few as ten trains connected Ipswich and Saxmundham daily. Only two trains now stopped at Westerfield while, conversely, two did not stop at Wickham Market.

In 1999 this level had continued virtually unchanged for thirty years, except for a brief period in the early 1990s when the number of trains rose to fourteen but had since fallen back to eleven. However, in 1999, all trains called at all stations, including the reinstated Melton.

Framlingham Branch

Trains started and finished their daily round at Framlingham, and, throughout its 93 year life, winter or summer, the branch did not see more than six, nor less than four, daily trains, all calling at both Parham and Marlesford and, after its opening in 1924, at Hacheston Halt. With so few trains, it is not really surprising that efforts were generally made to provide reasonably good connections in both directions with the main line services, usually involving a wait of well under an hour at Wickham Market. The precise timings over the years were, no doubt, due to changing social and travelling habits and, in some cases, to pressures exerted by the local gentry, businessmen or politicians. Of the timetables consulted, that for May 1860 had the earliest departure from the terminus, at 6.40 am, while that for Winter 1951/52 had the latest arrival back, at 8.26 pm.

June 1951

WICKHAM MARKET and FRAMLINGHAM

Miles	Week Days only	a.m	a.m		p.m	p.m		
	3 London (L'pool St.)..dep	4 35	10K30	..	3 33	5 30	..	..
—	Wickham Market B.. dep	9 40	1 25	..	6 9	8 0	..	..
1¾	Marlesford	9 46	1 31	..	6 15	8 6	..	..
2¾	Hacheston Halt	9 53	1 38	..	6 22	8 13	..	..
4	Parham Halt	9 59	1 41	..	6 28	8 19	..	..
6½	Framlingham.........arr	10 6	1 51	..	6 35	8 26	..	..

Miles	Week Days only	a.m		p.m S	p.m E	p.m	p.m
	Framlingham.........dep	8 38	..	1237	1247	3 20	6 52
2¼	Parham Halt	8 45	..	1244	1254	3 27	6 59
3¾	Hacheston Halt	8 48	..	1247	1257	3 30	7 2
4¾	Marlesford	8 56	..	1255	1 5	3 38	7 10
6½	Wickham Market B .. arr	9 1	..	1 0	1 10	3 43	7 15
91	3 London (L'pool St.). arr	11Y34	..	3Y11	4 0	6 48	9 46

B Station for Campsea Ashe E Except Saturdays K Dep. 10 40 a.m. on Saturdays S Saturdays only
V Arr. 4 0 p.m. on 23rd June and 22nd September from 27th July to 8th September inclusive Y Arr. 11 30 a.m. on Fridays and 11 27 a.m. on Saturdays

Tickets from Marlesford, Hacheston Halt, and Parham Halt are issued on the train.
Passengers to and from Hacheston Halt must join, or alight from, the special car provided

January 1921

LONDON, IPSWICH, BECCLES, LOWESTOFT, and YARMOUTH.—Great Eastern.

Down. Week Days.

Miles	Down	mrn	mrn	mrn		mrn	mrn	aft	aft (Except Saturdays)	aft (Saturdays only)
	234London(LpoolSt.)dp	....	5 0	....	....	8 15	10 0	....	....	1230
	234Chelmsford .... "	....	5 47	....	....	9 3	1050	....	....	1 28
	234Colchester ..... "	....	6 23	7 40	....	9 40	1128	....	....	1 12
—	Ipswich..........dep.	....	7 7	8 45	....	1032	12 2	1215		2 11
3¼	Westerfield	....	7 16	8 54	....	1041	....	....		....
7¼	Bealings	....	7 23	9 1	....	1048	....	....		....
10¾	Woodbridge	....	7 30	9 7	....	1055	....	1233		....
11¾	Melton	....	7 34	9 11	....	1059	....	....		....
15¾	Wickham Market ‖ 237	....	7 46	9 21	....	1110	....	1245		....
22¼	Saxmundham 233	....	8 0	9 33	....	1123	1235	1257		2 44
26¾	Darsham, for Yoxford	....	8 10	9 43	....	1133	....	1 8		....
32	Halesworth 239a	....	8 24	9 54	....	1145	1252	1 20		3 1
36	Brampton	....	8 33	10 3	....	1154	....	....		....
40½	Beccles 240........arr.	....	8 42	1012	....	12 3	1 7	1 35		3 16
—	Beccles ....dep.	7 5	8 56	1035	....	1220	1 20	1 43	3 10	3 25
47	Carlton Colville	7 16	9 8	1046	....	1232	1 31	1 54	3 21	3 36
49	Lowestoft (C.) †..arr.	7 22	9 14	1052	....	1238	1 37	2 2	3 27	3 42
—	Beccles ....dep.	....	8 46	1026	....	12 6	1 11	1 38	....	3 20
43¾	Aldeby	....	8 55	1029	....	1215	....	1 47	....	....
46	Haddiscoe 250 .....arr.	....	8 59	1033	....	1219	....	1 51	....	....
61¾	250Norwich (T.) ..arr.	....	9 47	1217	....	1 45	....	2 54	....	....
—	Haddiscoe.........dep.	....	9 0	1034	....	1220	....	1 52	....	....
46½	St. Olaves	....	9 5	1039	....	1225	....	1 57	....	....
49	Belton ....[271, 272	....	9 11	1045	....	1231	....	2 3	....	....
53	Yarmouth (S. Tn.)..arr.	....	9 21	1055	....	1240	1 36	2 12	....	3 45

Miles	Down	aft	aft (Tuesdays only)	aft (Fridays only)	aft	aft	aft	aft (Restaurant Cars, London to Yarmouth)	aft	aft (Restaurant Cars, London to Lowestoft)		
	234London(LpoolSt.)dp	1230	....	....	3 10	....	3 20	4 55	5 23	7 45	....	....
	234Chelmsford .... "	1 28	....	....	3 3	....	4 5	4 30	....	8 29	....	....
	234Colchester ..... "	1V39	....	....	3 53	....	4 36	5 22	....	9 12	....	....
—	Ipswich..........dep.	2 21	4 15		4 50	....	5 9	6 28	7 11	9 46	....	....
3¼	Westerfield	2 30	4 24		....	....	5 18	....	7 20	....	....	....
7¼	Bealings	2 37	4 31		....	....	5 25	....	7 27	....	....	....
10¾	Woodbridge	2 44	4 37		....	....	5 33	6 46	7 34	10 3	....	....
11¾	Melton	2 48	4 41		....	....	5 37	....	7 39	10 7	....	....
15¾	Wickham Market ‖ 237	2 59	4 52		....	....	5 49	6 58	7 52	1017	....	....
22¼	Saxmundham 233	3 12	5 2		....	....	6 4	7 11	8 5	1028	....	....
26¾	Darsham, for Yoxford	3 22			....	....	6 14	....	8 16	1038	....	....
32	Halesworth 239a	3 36			....	....	6 28	7 28	8 30	1049	....	....
36	Brampton	3 45			....	....	6 37	....	8 39	....	....	....
40½	Beccles 240........arr.	3 54			5 45	....	6 46	7 43	8 48	11 4	....	....
—	Beccles ....dep.	4 6		4 50	5 53	....	6 57	7 53	8 55	1111	....	....
47	Carlton Colville	4 17		5 1	6 4	....	7 8	8 4	9 6	....	....	....
49	Lowestoft (C.) †..arr.	4 23		5 7	6 10	....	7 14	8 10	9 12	1126	....	....
—	Beccles ....dep.	3 57		....	5 49	6 0	6 52	7 47	8 51	11 7	....	....
43¾	Aldeby	4 6		....	....	6 9	7 1	....	9 0	....	....	....
46	Haddiscoe 250 .....arr.	4 10		....	....	6 13	7 5	....	9 4	....	....	....
61¾	250Norwich (T.) ..arr.	6 19	....	....	....	....	8 35	....	9 52	....	....	....
—	Haddiscoe.........dep.	4 11	....	....	....	6 14	7 6	....	9 5	....	....	....
46½	St. Olaves	4 16	....	....	....	6 19	7 11	....	9 10	....	....	....
49	Belton ....[271, 272	4 22	....	....	....	6 26	7 17	....	9 16	....	....	....
53	Yarmouth (S. Tn.)..arr.	4 31	....	....	6 15	6 35	7 26	8 12	9 25	1132	....	....

Miles	Down (Sundays)	mrn	mrn	mrn	aft	aft	
	234London(LpoolSt.)dp	....	....	9 15	....	4 25	....
	234Chelmsford .... "	....	....	10 5	....	4 28	....
	234Colchester ..... "	....	....	1043	....	5 40	....
—	Ipswich..........dep.	....	9 0	1127	....	6 17	....
3¼	Westerfield	....	9 9	....	....	6 27	....
7¼	Bealings	....	9 17	....	....	6 35	....
10¾	Woodbridge	....	9 24	1145	....	6 43	....
11¾	Melton	....	9 28	....	....	6 47	....
15¾	Wickham Market ‖ 237	....	9 38	1157	....	6 58	....
22¼	Saxmundham 233	....	9 50	1210	....	7 11	....
26¾	Darsham, for Yoxford	....	10 0	1221	....	7 23	....
32	Halesworth 239a	....	1011	1234	....	7 36	....
36	Brampton	....	1020	....	....	7 46	....
40½	Beccles 240........arr.	....	1029	1247	....	7 55	....
—	Beccles ....dep.	7 50	1036	1256	6 26	8 3	....
47	Carlton Colville	8 1	1047	1 8	6 37	8 14	....
49	Lowestoft (C.) †..arr.	8 7	1053	1 14	6 43	8 20	....
—	Beccles ....dep.	....	1032	1250	....	7 59	....
43¾	Aldeby	....	1041	....	....	8 11	....
46	Haddiscoe 250 .....arr.	....	....	1 2	....	....	....
61¾	250Norwich (T.) ..arr.	....	....	2 14	....	....	....
—	Haddiscoe.........dep.	....	....	1 3	....	....	....
46½	St. Olaves	....	1049	....	....	8 19	....
49	Belton ....[271, 272	....	1056	....	....	8 26	....
53	Yarmouth (S. Tn.)..arr.	....	11 4	1 22	....	8 35	....

LONDON, IPSWICH, SAXMUNDHAM, BECCLES, LOWESTOFT, and YARMOUTH.

Miles	Down.	Week Days. mrn	mrn (Tuesdays only.)	mrn		mrn	mrn (Saturdays only.)		mrn	mrn		aft (Sats. only.)	aft	aft (Tuesdays only.)		aft	aft	aft	S	E	aft (Wednesdays and Saturdays.)			Sundays. mrn	mrn		aft
	Liverpool Street, 856London ......dep.	5 0	..	..	..	8 15	8 45	..	10 3	..	..	1225	..	..	..	310	3 15	4R55	5 18	5 18	7 42	..	..	..	9 15	..	4 35
—	**Ipswich**..........dep.	7 7	8 20	8 55	..	10 38	11 30	..	12 3	1220	..	2 0	2 20	4 15	..	450	5 9	6 28	7 14	7 12	9 45	..	..	9 20	1132	..	6 36
3¾	Westerfield..........	7 16	..	9 4	..	10 47	11 39	..	..	..	..	..	2 29	4 24	..	..	5 18	..	7 23	7 21	9 54	..	..	9 29	..	..	6 45
7¼	Bealings..........	7 23	8 33	9 11	..	10 54	11 46	..	..	1234	..	..	2 36	4 31	..	..	5 25	..	7 30	7 28	10 1	..	..	9 36	..	..	6 52
10½	Woodbridge	7 30	8 39	9 18	..	11 0	11 52	..	..	1241	..	..	2 43	4 37	..	..	5 32	6 46	7 36	7 35	10 7	..	..	9 42	1148	..	6 58
11¾	Melton..........[874	7 34	8 43	9 22	..	11 4	11 56	..	..	1245	..	..	2 47	4 41	..	..	5 36	..	7 40	7 40	1011	..	..	9 47	..	..	7 2
15¾	Wickham Market A	7 46	8 53	9 31	..	11 14	12 6	..	..	1255	..	..	2 57	4 51	..	..	5 47	6 58	7 50	7 51	1020	..	..	9 58	1159	..	7 12
22½	**Saxmundham 874**...	8 0	9 4	9 42	..	11 25	12 15	..	1234	1 6	..	2 31	3 9	5 0	..	..	6 0	7 11	8 0	8 2	1029	..	..	1010	1210	..	7 24
26¾	Darsham, for Yoxford	8 10	9 13	9 51	..	11 34		..	..	1 17	..	..	3 18		..	..	6 9	..	8 9	8 13		..	..	1020	1219	..	7 33
32	Halesworth ¶.........	8 24	9 22	10 1	..	11 45		..	1250	1 30	..	2 46	3 31		..	..	6 22	7 28	8 19	8 25		..	..	1032	1230	..	7 44
36	Brampton (Suffolk)...	8 33		1010	..	11 53		..	..	1 39	..	..	3 40		..	..	6 31	..	8 28	8 34		..	..	1043	..	..	7 54
40½	**Beccles 875** ......arr.	8 45		1018	..	12 1		..	1 3	1 50	..	2 59	3 48		..	541	6 40	7 43	8 36	8 42		..	..	1051	1243	..	8 2
49	**Lowestoft**(C.) B arr.	9 17		1054	..	12 26		..	1 37	2 21	..	3 24	4 23		..	6 6	7 7	8 8	9 7	9 7		..	..	1117	1 12	..	8 28
—	**Beccles** ....dep.	8 50		1027	..	12 5		..	1 8	1 55	..	3 3	3 52		..	545	6 46	7 47	8 40	8 46		..	..	1055	1247	..	8 6
43¾	Aldeby	8 58		1035	..	12 13		..	..	2 3	..		4 2		..	..	6 54	..	8 48	8 56		..	..	11 4	..	..	8 14
46	Haddiscoe **884, 885**..	9 1		1038	..	12 16		..	1 16	..	..		4 5		..	..	6 57	7 56	8 51	..		..	..	..	..	..	..
61½	**885**Norwich (Th.) arr.	9 48		1217	..	1A11		..	2 44	..	..		5A25	..	..	..	8 23	9 50	9 50	..		..	..	..	..	..	..
46¾	St. Olaves.......[**1083**	9 5	..	1042	..	12 20		..	..	2 9	..		4 9	..	..	..	7 1	..	8 55	9 2		..	..	1110	..	..	8 20
49	Belton & Burgh[**1082**,	9 11	....	1048	..	12 26		..	..	2 15	..		4 15	..	..	..	7 7	..	9 1	9 8		..	..	1116	..	..	8 26
53	**Yarmouth** (S. T.) arr.	9 20	..	1055	..	12 33		..	1 31	2 22	..	3 25	4 22	..	..	6 7	7 14	8 11	9 8	9 15		..	..	1123	1 9	..	8 33

A Station 2 miles distant at Campsea Ash.

A One class only.

B Station for Kessingland; frequent service of Motors.

E Except Sats.

R Restaurant Car, Liverpool St. to Yarmouth (South Town).

S or **S** Sats. only.

V Except Mons.

November 1930

November 1966

			WEEKDAYS												SUNDAYS		
													T					
RAIL	London Liverpool Street	d	....	04 30	07 00	09 30	11 30	13 30	....	14 30	15 30	....	16 50	....	18 30	12 30	16 30	17 30
	Ipswich	a	..	06 40	08 46	10 39	12 39	14 39	..	15 50	16 39	..	18 10	..	19 50	13 58	17 50	18 42
	Ipswich	d	....	**06 52**	**08 52**	**10 52**	**12 52**	**14 52**	....	**16 22**	**16 56**	**17 36**	**18 11**	....	**19 57**	**14 05**	**18 05**	**18 50**
	Westerfield	d	..	..	**08 58**	**10 58**	**12 58**	**14 53**	..	..	..	..	..	..	..	**14 11**	**18 11**	**18 56**
	Woodbridge	d	....	**07 09**	**09 10**	**11 10**	**13 10**	**15 10**	....	**16 38**	**17 16**	**17 53**	**18 30**	....	**20 15**	**14 23**	**18 23**	**19 08**
	Wickham Market	d	..	..	**09 18**	**11 18**	**13 18**	**15 18**	..	**16 46**	**17 26**	**18 01**	..	..	**20 23**	**14 31**	**18 31**	**19 16**
	Saxmundham	a	....	**07 24**	**09 26**	**11 26**	**13 26**	**15 26**	....	**16 55**	**17 38**	**18 09**	**18 48**	....	**20 31**	**14 39**	**18 39**	**19 24**
BUS	Saxmundham *	d	..	..	..	..	..	**15e52**	..	..	17 52	..	..	..	21 37	15 52	19 20	20 30
	Saxmundham (Rail Station)	d	....	07 36	09 36	11 36	13 36	....	....	17 06	....	....	18 56	....	....	....	....	....
	Leiston (PO Square) ..	a	..	07 51	09 51	11 51	13 51	**16e07**	..	17 21	18 16	..	19 11	..	22 01	16 16	19 35	20 45
	Aldeburgh (High Street) ..	a	....	08 07	10 07	12 07	14 07	**16e28**	....	17 37	18 32	....	19 27	....	22 17	16 32	19 51	21 01
RAIL	Saxmundham	d	..	**07 24**	**09 27**	**11 27**	**13 27**	**15 27**	..	..	**17 38**	**18 11**	**18 49**	..	**20 32**	**14 40**	**18 40**	**19 25**
	Darsham	d	....	**07 32**	**09 34**	**11 34**	**13 34**	**15 34**	....	....	**17 47**	**18 18**	....	....	**20 39**	**14 47**	**18 47**	**19 32**
	Halesworth	d	**06 26**	**07 53**	**09 43**	**11 43**	**13 43**	**15 43**	**17 02**	..	**17 57**	**18 28**	**19 05**	**19 41**	**20 48**	**14 56**	**18 56**	**19 41**
	Brampton	d	**06 34**	**08 00**	**09 50**	**11 50**	**13 50**	**15 50**	**17 09**	....	....	**18 35**	....	**19 48**	**20 55**	**15 03**	**19 03**	**19 48**
	Beccles	d	**06 45**	**08 08**	**09 58**	**11 58**	**13 58**	**15 58**	**17 18**	..	**18 12**	**18 43**	**19 20**	**19 56**	**21 03**	**15 11**	**19 11**	**19 59**
	Oulton Broad South	d	**06 57**	**08 18**	**10 08**	**12 08**	**14 08**	**16 08**	**17 28**	....	....	**18 53**	**19 32**	**20 06**	**21 13**	**15 21**	**19 21**	**20 09**
	Lowestoft Central	a	**07 03**	**08 23**	**10 13**	**12 13**	**14 13**	**16 13**	**17 34**	..	**18 27**	**18 58**	**19 38**	**20 11**	**21 18**	**15 26**	**19 26**	**20 14**

a—Arrival time b—20 minutes later on Saturdays d—departure time
e—On Saturdays departs Saxmundham 16 45, arrives Leiston 17 00 and Aldeburgh 17 16
T—Through train (First and Second Class) between Liverpool Street and Lowestoft Central — Snacks and drinks available
*—Eastern Counties Omnibus Co. Garage

Fares from November 1966, together with the cheery logo that was introduced in 1974.

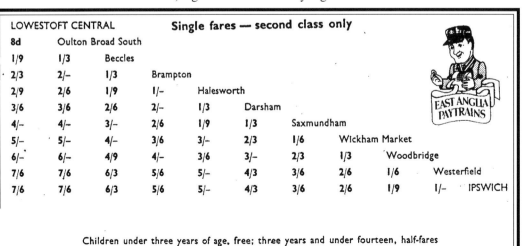

LOWESTOFT CENTRAL **Single fares — second class only**

8d	Oulton Broad South									
1/9	**1/3**	Beccles								
2/3	**2/-**	**1/3**	Brampton							
2/9	**2/6**	**1/9**	**1/-**	Halesworth						
3/6	**3/6**	**2/6**	**2/-**	**1/3**	Darsham					
4/-	**4/-**	**3/-**	**2/6**	**1/9**	**1/3**	Saxmundham				
5/-	**5/-**	**4/-**	**3/6**	**3/-**	**2/3**	**1/6**	Wickham Market			
6/-	**6/-**	**4/9**	**4/-**	**3/6**	**3/-**	**2/3**	**1/3**	Woodbridge		
7/6	**7/6**	**6/3**	**5/6**	**5/-**	**4/3**	**3/6**	**2/6**	**1/6**	Westerfield	
7/6	**7/6**	**6/3**	**5/6**	**5/-**	**4/3**	**3/6**	**2/6**	**1/9**	**1/-**	IPSWICH

Children under three years of age, free; three years and under fourteen, half-fares

1. Ipswich to Wickham Market Junction

IPSWICH

1. "The Easterling" express from Liverpool Street to Yarmouth and Lowestoft negotiates the points at the north end of the station behind Class B17 4-6-0 no. 61668 *Bradford City* on 1st July 1952. Running non-stop between London and Beccles, this train appeared in the summer timetables from 1950 to 1958, and provided the East Suffolk line with a named express during an era when such names reflected the prestige of a route. (H.N.James/J.Day)

2. Experimental 4-wheel railbus LEV 1 stands at platform 4b on a wet November morning in 1980 prior to working the 10.48 to Lowestoft. It ran trials over the line for some two months, but the absence of toilet and luggage facilities counted against it over such a long journey, and the East Suffolk route remained the haunt of conventional diesel units until the Sprinters arrived in the late 1980s. (B.Harrison)

3. The station was electrified and resignalled during the mid-1980s. These modifications are evident as a train of nuclear flasks, bound for Sizewell on the former Aldeburgh branch, waits to continue its journey north over the East Suffolk line. (H.N.James/J.Day)

4. In 1911/12 a second pair of tracks was laid between the station and East Suffolk Junction, thus allowing Norwich and East Suffolk traffic to run separately between these points. With the Norwich lines in the foreground, class D16 4-4-0s nos. 62544 and 62521 double-head a train from the East Suffolk line towards the station on 21st May 1950. (K.A.Leighton)

EAST SUFFOLK JUNCTION

The arrangement of the junction prior to the 1911/1912 alterations is shown in this plan dating from1904. The extensive Railway Civil Engineer's depot which later occupied the whole area on the east side of the line between London Road and Hadleigh Road bridges had yet to be built.

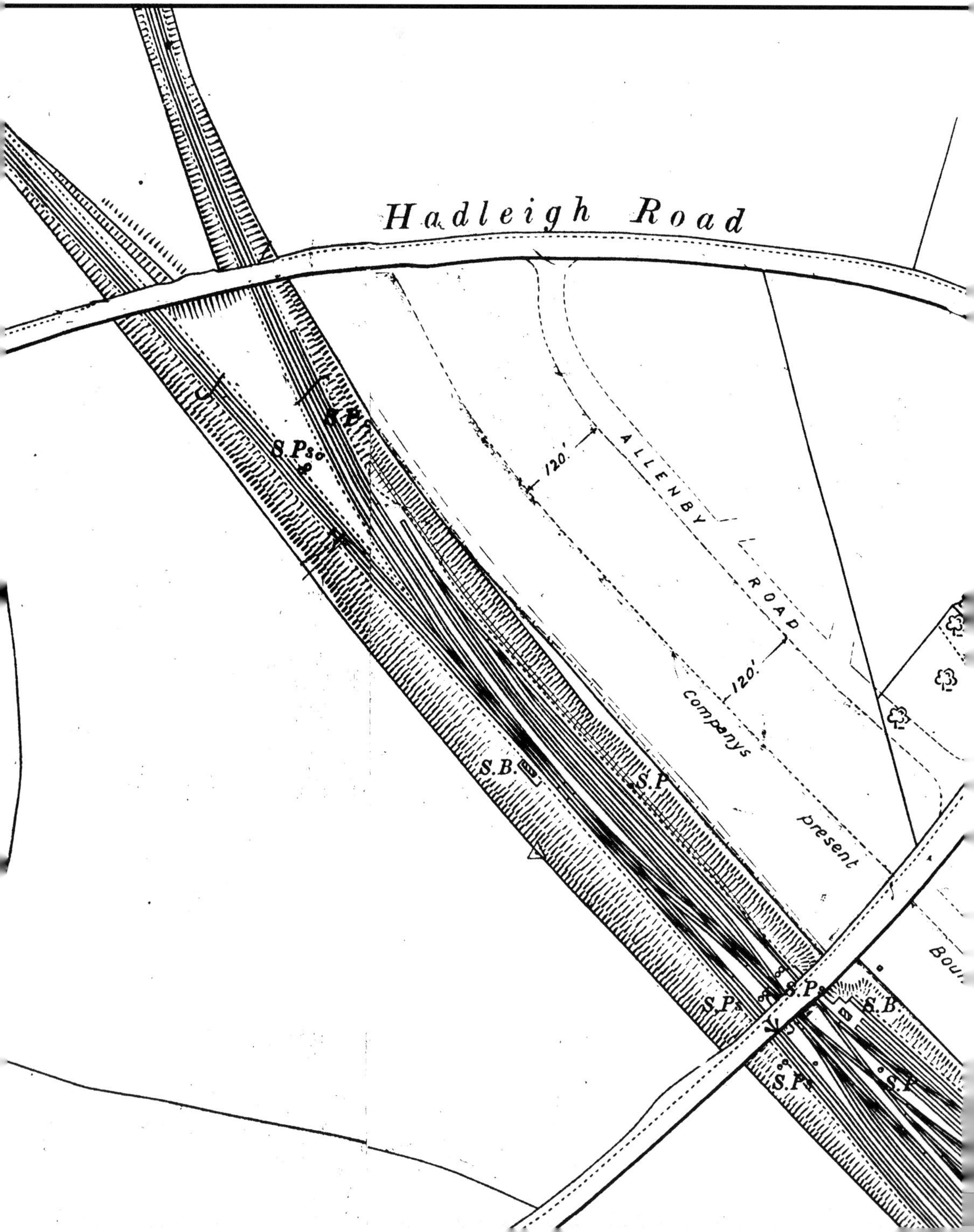

5. Just under a mile north of the station, the Yarmouth line diverged from the route to Bury and Norwich at the aptly named East Suffolk Junction. Here is the junction looking north before the 1911 alterations, with the Norwich line continuing straight ahead under the road bridge. (National Railway Museum)

6. By the mid 1970s, the scene had changed greatly – the west side of the cutting had been widened to accommodate the extra pair of tracks which became the Norwich line, whilst the opposite side had been levelled in the 1930s to allow for the creation of Ipswich engineers yard. A class 37 heads an up express from the East Suffolk line, over the original alignment, and despite the changes, a comparison with the previous photograph will reveal striking similarities in the track layout. (H.N.James/J.Day)

NORTH OF EAST SUFFOLK JUNCTION

In this 1928 plan the detailed layout of the premises and private sidings to the north-east of Hadleigh Road bridge is clearly shown. Petters (Ipswich) Ltd. owned the premises shown as "Ipswich Works" while the "Handford Works" belonged to the Manganese Bronze & Brass Co. Ltd. The "Seed Cleaning Warehouse" was later to become the Eastern Counties Farmers Ltd. premises

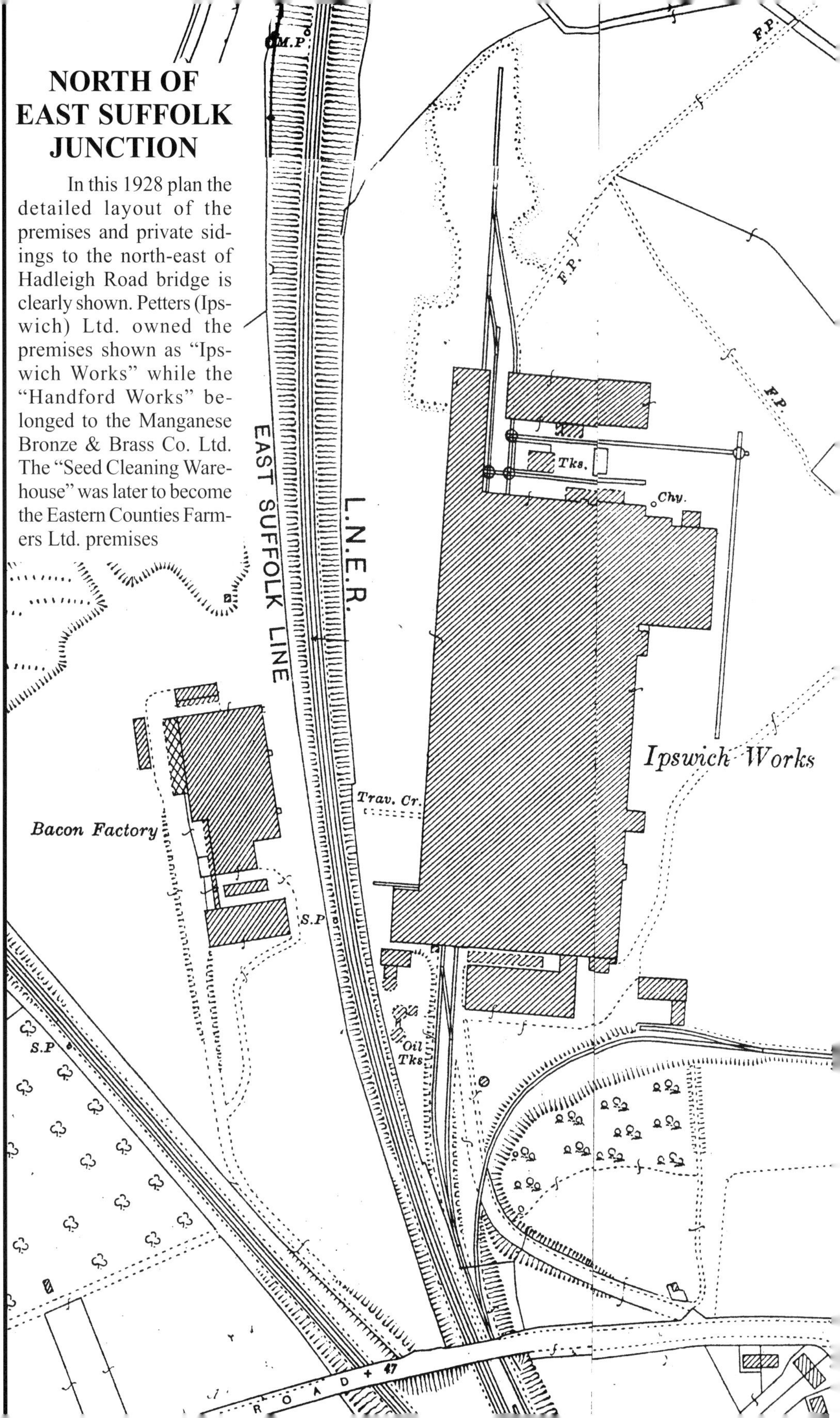

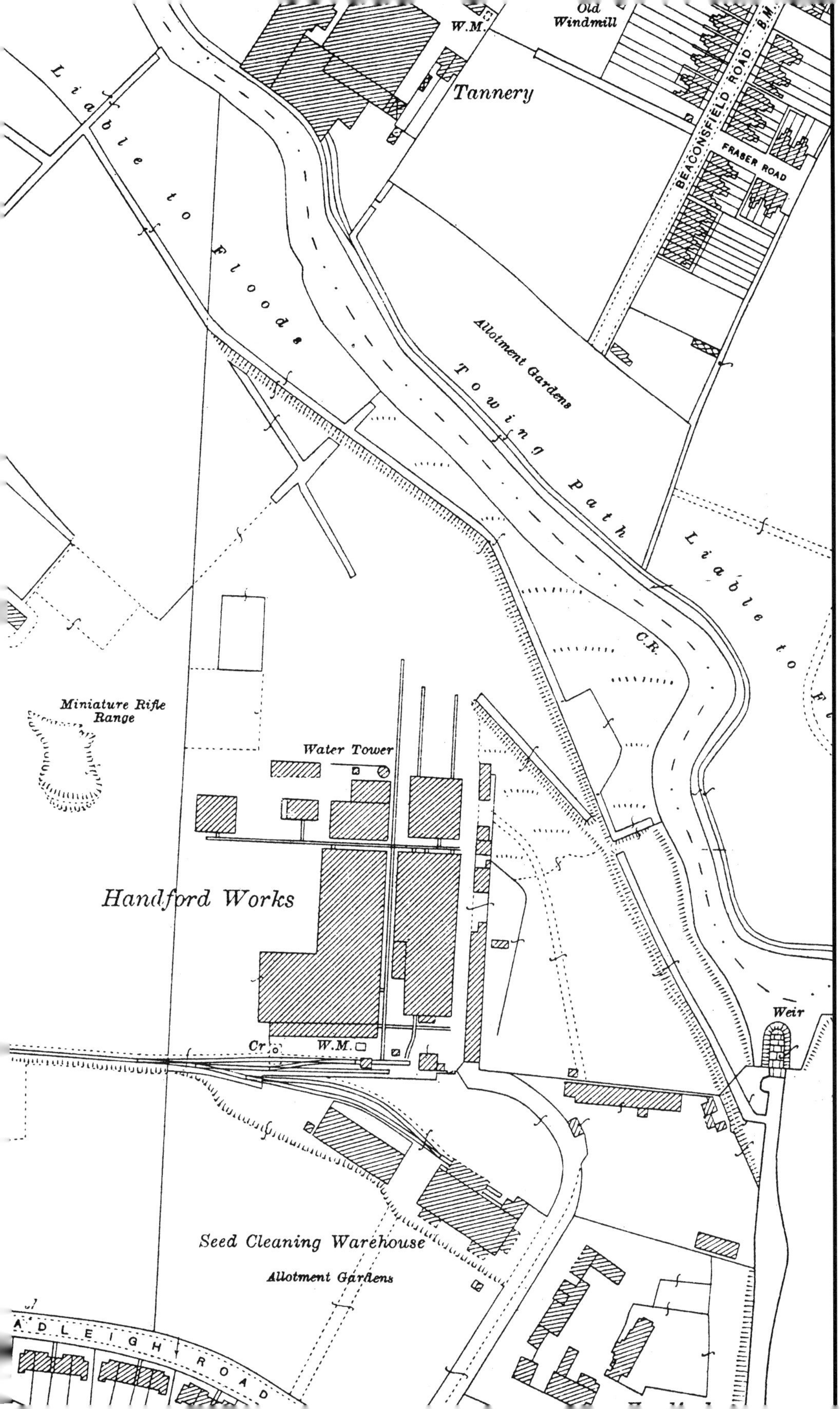
Old Windmill
W.M.
Tannery
BEACONSFIELD ROAD
B.M.
FRASER ROAD
Liable to Floods
Allotment Gardens
Towing Path
C.R.
Miniature Rifle Range
Water Tower
Handford Works
Weir
Cr.
W.M.
Seed Cleaning Warehouse
Allotment Gardens
ROAD

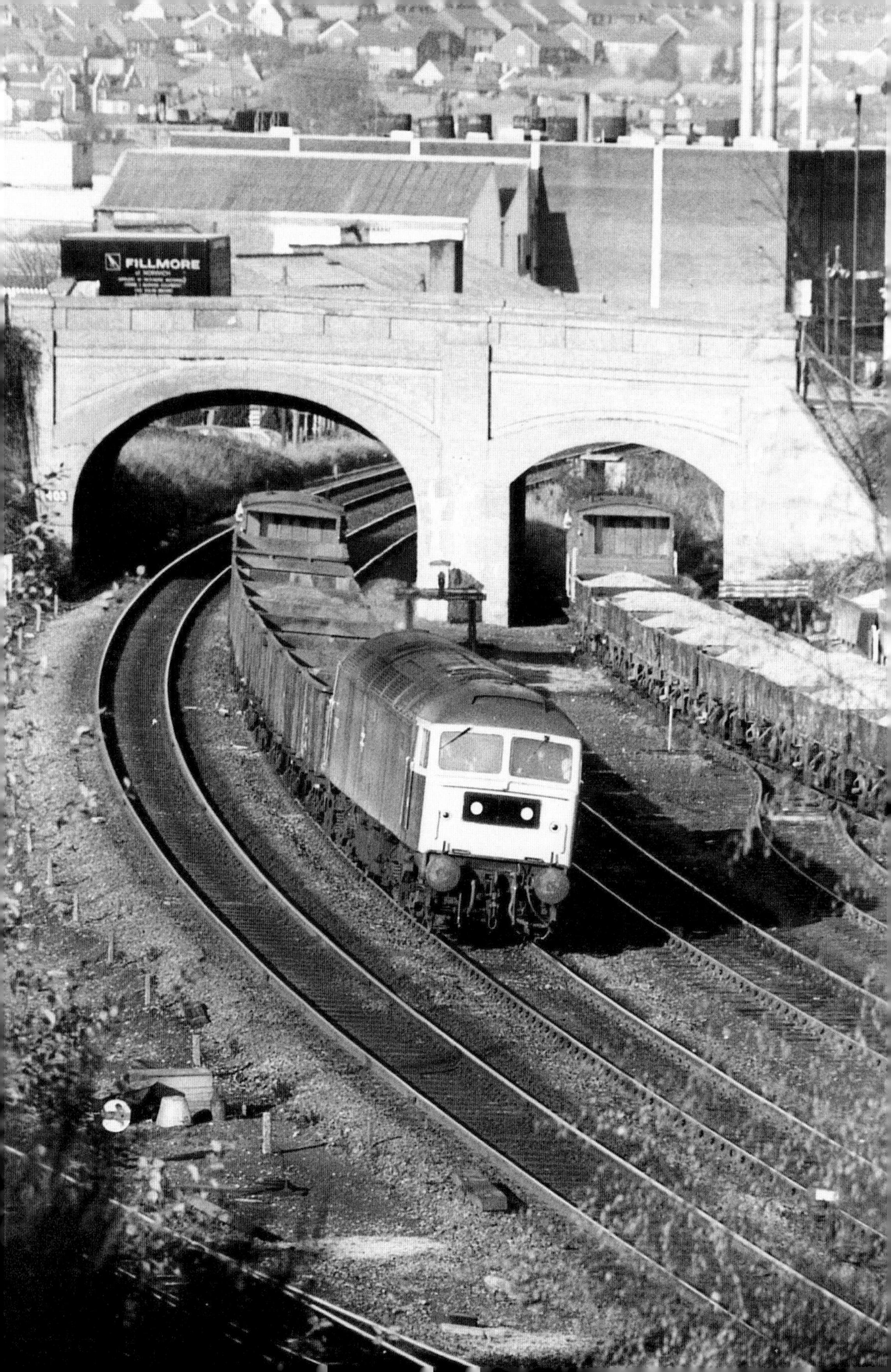
FILLMORE

←

7. 47007 comes under Hadleigh Road bridge with a goods train from Derby Road on 24th November 1982. The small arch of the bridge, now spanning no more than a headshunt from the engineers yard, was once the access to a fascinating but little known complex of private sidings. (I.Cowley)

8. We now pause in our journey down the East Suffolk line for a look at these lines and some of the engines that worked on them. *Neptune*, a Manning Wardle 0-4-0ST, approaches Hadleigh Road bridge with wagons for Petters Ltd private siding in the late 1920s. It is running parallel to the double track East Suffolk line, with the Norwich line beyond. (R.G.Pratt)

9. *Neptune* left Ipswich in August 1929 for Liverpool, where it was to be used in the construction of a sea wall. With the cab removed, it is seen here securely chained to a well wagon in Ipswich yard ready for the long journey north. (R.G.Pratt)

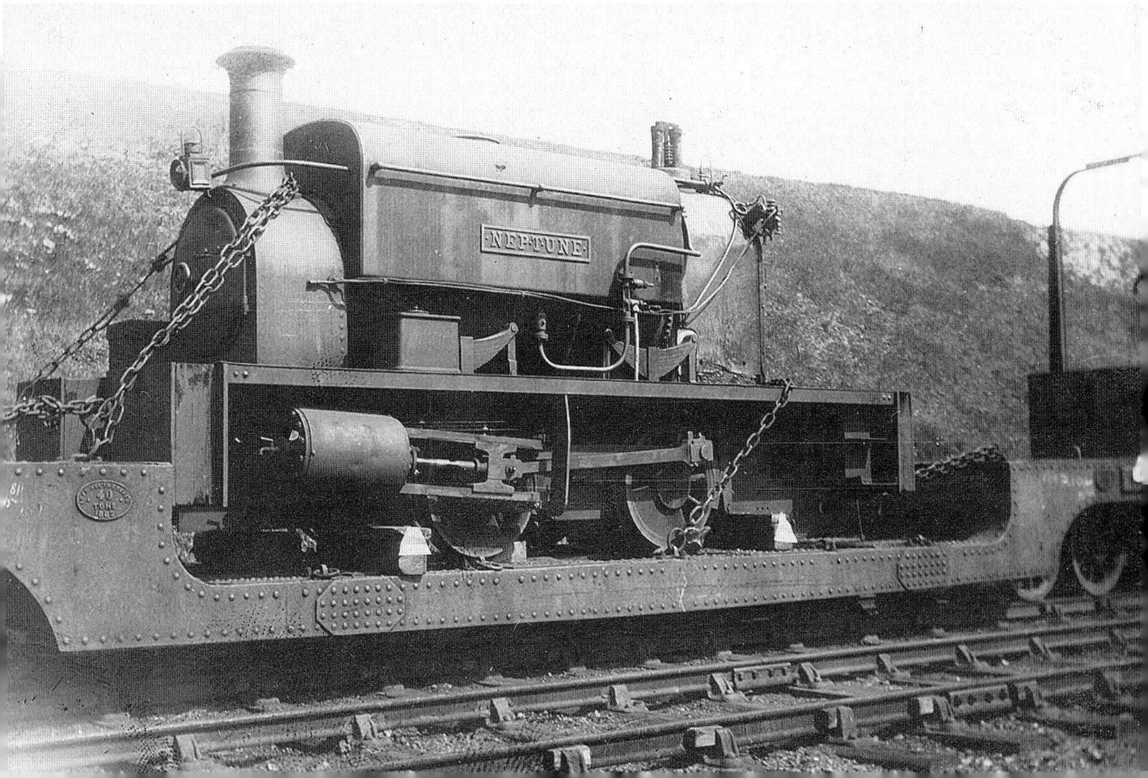

10. The Manganese Bronze and Brass Company factory was adjacent to that of Petters. It, too, operated Manning Wardle 0-4-0ST locomotives, and here we see *Percy*, dating from 1872, in a typical industrial railway setting. The lines branching off to the right of the picture lead to the "Seed Cleaning Warehouse" shown on the map. (R.G.Pratt)

11. *Percy* and its crew take a break from their shunting activities and pose for the photographer. The engine shed is on the right, whilst a steam lorry, framed by the ironwork behind the engine, adds to the interest of the scene. (R.G.Pratt)

12. *Percy* was scrapped in 1930 and was replaced by another Manning Wardle 0-4-0ST, *Philip*, which had been built in 1895 and survived until 1939. The younger locomotive is seen here shunting a patched-up private owner wagon in the sidings, with the Petters factory in the distance. (R.G.Pratt)

13. North of Hadleigh Road bridge, the East Suffolk line continues to curve sharply in a generally eastward direction. Class L1 2-6-4T no. 67706 drifts round towards the junction with a goods train from Felixstowe on 28th May 1953. On the extreme right of the picture the private siding serving the Manganese works curves round in front of the former Petters building. (H.N.James/J.Day)

14. Some fifteen years later, a class 31 was photographed at much the same spot with an up passenger train. The signal gantry confirms the location, but the surrounding area has changed greatly in a short while. Petters yard is given over to road transport, while a gasholder, rather than the spindly water tower, dominates the skyline. (H.N.James/J.Day)

15. Class J15 0-6-0 no. 65389 tackles the 1 in 111 gradient past the gasholder in fine style with the down Snape goods train on a grey winter morning in the late 1950s. (R.W.Smith)

16. Seconds later the photographer turns to his left to capture no. 65389 as it crosses the steel span of the bridge over the River Gipping. (R.W.Smith)

17. When this photograph was taken some seventy years earlier, the line was carried over the river at this point by a wooden trestle bridge. There is a more rural feel to the scene as a young man sits on the river bank, watching a GER 2-4-0 as it heads north over the river.
(H.Moffatt collection)

18. The line continues to climb on an embankment, offering views of the townscape of north-west Ipswich. No 37088 crosses the Norwich Road on 10th May 1984, at the head of the through train from Liverpool Street to Lowestoft. The "Ferodo" advertisement had been a distinctive feature of this bridge for many years. (H.N.James/J.Day)

19. Class N7 0-6-2T no. 9701, still bearing its LNER lettering and number, heads a train from Felixstowe through Henley Road bridge on 16th April 1950. The substantial engineering of this part of the line is again evident. (K.A.Leighton)

→

20. By the 1990s this had become the busiest section of the East Suffolk line, with an ever-expanding traffic to the Port of Felixstowe sharing the tracks with the passenger services to Felixstowe and Lowestoft. A train of freightliner flats from the port passes a loaded train heading in the opposite direction on Westerfield bank. (I.Cowley)

WESTERFIELD BRICKWORKS BRANCH

This 1904 plan, which is at 16 ins to 1 mile, shows a private railway that meandered its way from Westerfield yard through what was to become a largely residential area adjoining Henley Road and Dales Hall Lane (later Dales Road). It had been in existence for about forty years when the tracks were lifted in the mid 1920s. On the East Suffolk main line the location of Westerfield Bank signalbox, which opened in 1898 and closed in 1926, can also be seen due north of the western extremity of the branch.

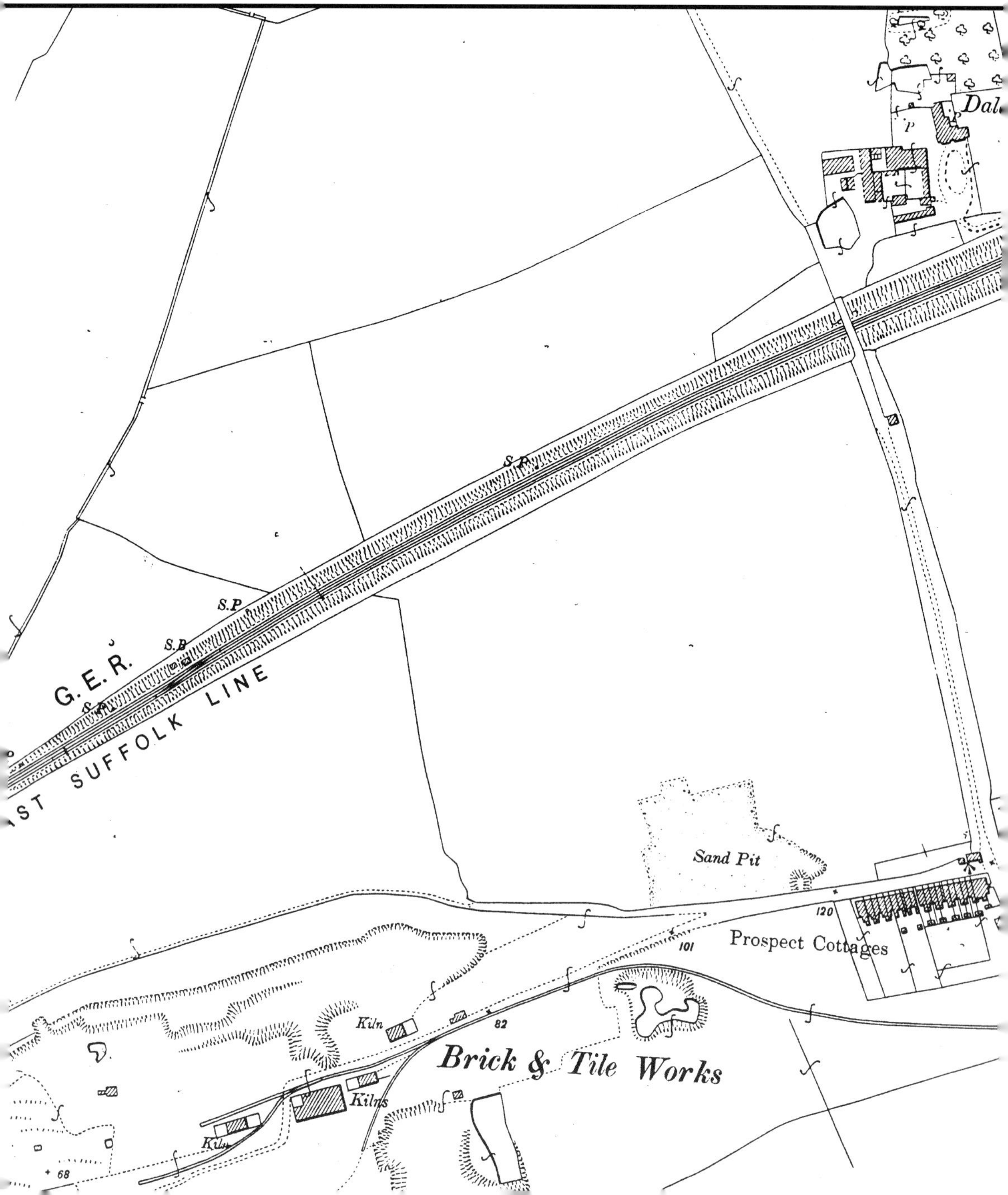

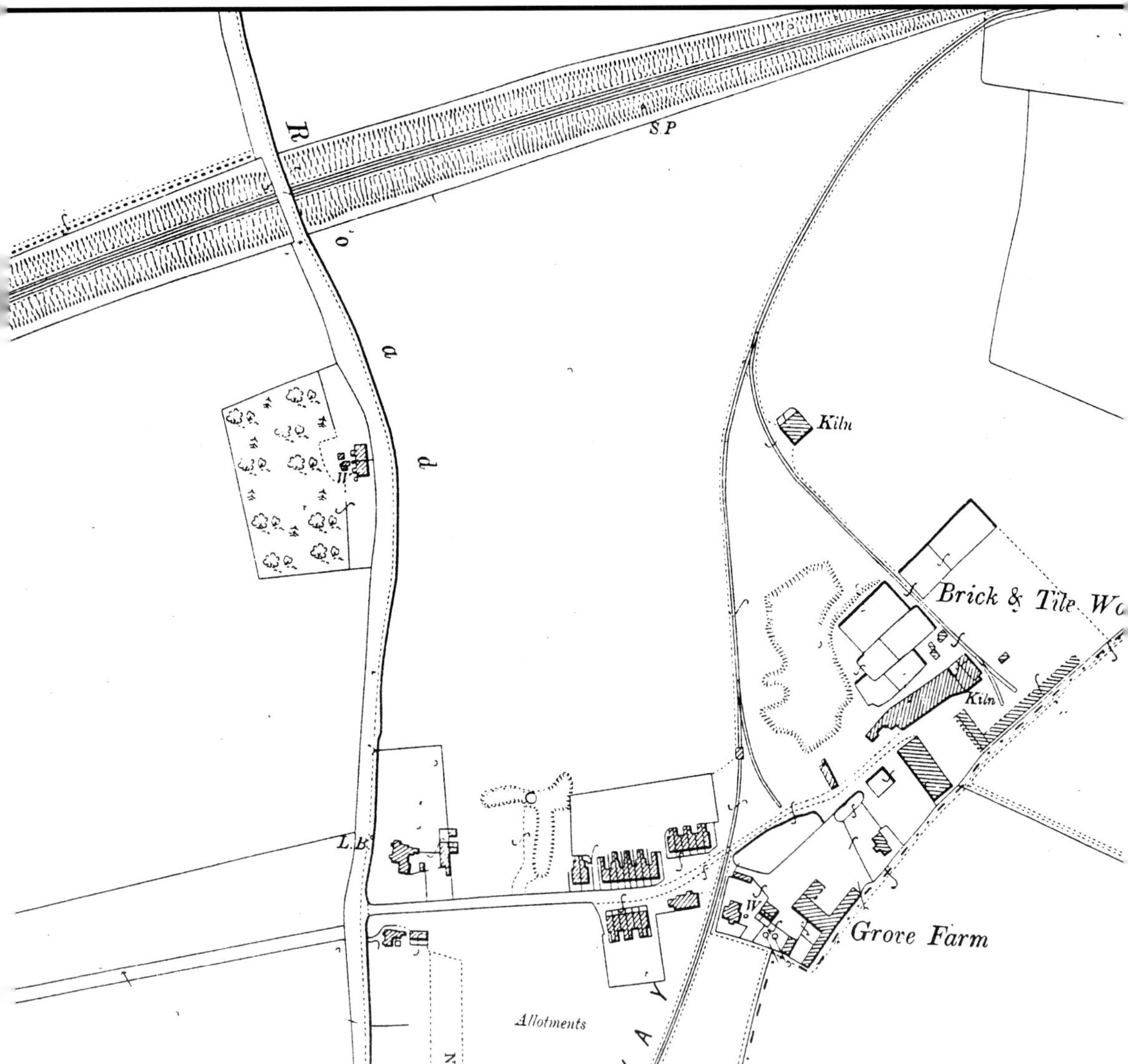

Road
S.P
Kiln
Brick & Tile Wo
Kiln
L.B
W
Grove Farm
Allotments
Nursery
RAILWAY

WESTERFIELD

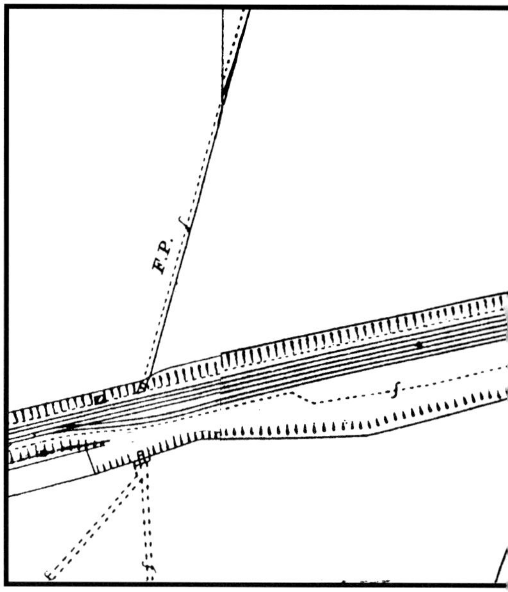

This 1928 plan shows the platforms built for the privately promoted Felixstowe Dock & Railway Company and opened in 1877. The GER began to work the branch in 1879, from which date the platforms saw relatively little use for passenger purposes. The tracks remained in these platforms until the mid 1960s, at which time all sidings were removed following withdrawal of freight facilities on 13th July 1964. The branch to the brickworks left the yard in the bottom left-hand corner, but had been removed by the time the area was surveyed for this plan.

21. Looking west over the level crossing in 1911, the photographer has captured a quiet morning in Westerfield yard, although the crossing gates are open and the signal is cleared for the passage of an up train. By the gate, a horse waits patiently while its owner unloads coal from a railway wagon. At the far end of the yard we obtain a rare glimpse of the line which served the Dales Road brickworks, a mile or so distant. Another little-known Ipswich industrial line, it was lifted by 1927 after some years of disuse. (National Railway Museum)

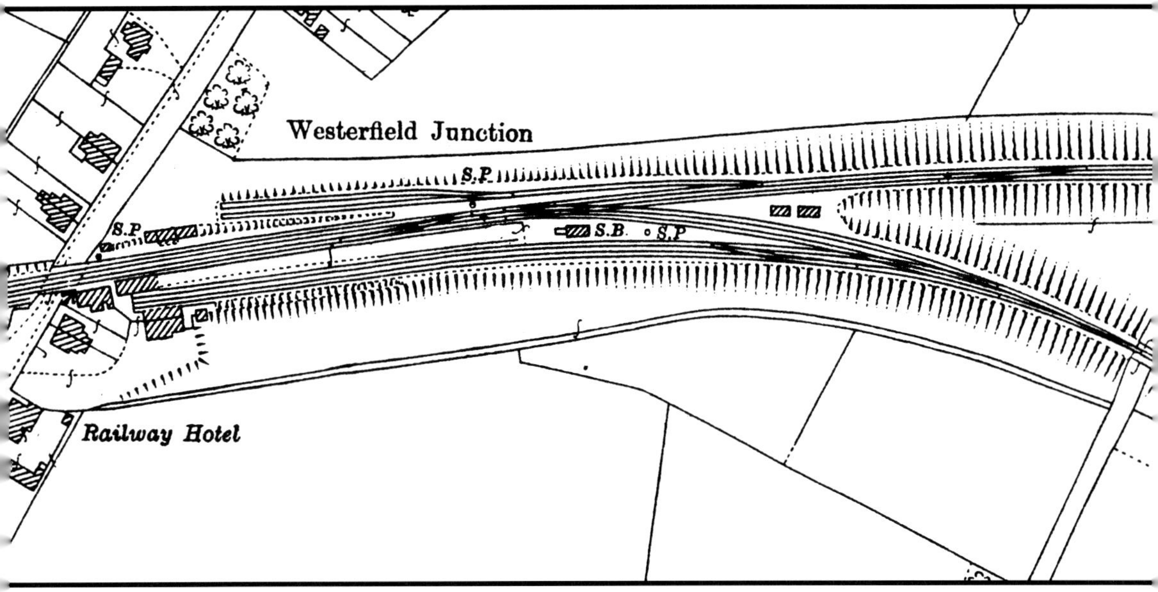

22. B17 4-6-0 no.61656 *Leeds United* passes the point where the brickworks line diverged as it heads for Ipswich with a milk train on 22nd May 1957. Such trains, serving the dairy at Halesworth, were a regular sight on the line for many years. (R.C.Riley)

23. On 25th September 1900 a goods train from Ipswich was waiting at the signal south of the level crossing when the boiler of the locomotive, Y14 0-6-0 no. 522 exploded, killing the crew. Shortly after the accident, railway staff inspect the remains of the loco - the train itself appears unscathed by the incident. By tragic coincidence, the son of the driver was also killed in a railway accident, at Colchester some 13 years later. (HMRS)

24. This view, looking in a generally westerly direction, clearly shows the layout as it was in 1911. The Felixstowe Dock & Railway Company station is on the left, with the East Suffolk platforms in the centre of the picture. (National Railway Museum)

25. Looking east from the down starter signal in 1911, we see a "Claud Hamilton" 4-4-0 standing on the Felixstowe line, whilst a platelayers trolley occupies the up main. Two years later a replacement signal box was built adjacent to the signal in the foreground, thus improving visibility for the signalman. (National Railway Museum)

70007

26. "Britannia" 4-6-2 no.70007 *Coeur de Lion* heads an up East Suffolk line express through the deserted station one day in 1959. By this time these powerful engines were becoming a common sight on the line as the diesels infiltrated the Norwich expresses. (Stations UK)

27. A Cravens DMU heads for Ipswich on 11th September 1969. The tracks in the Felixstowe Dock & Railway Company platforms have been lifted, but the weather-boarded building, with its distinctive roof, survives. (National Railway Museum)

28. "Sprinter" no.150213, working a train from Lowestoft, passes the simplified junction on 30th January 1999. The notice and the aerial protruding from the roof of the signal box provide evidence of the radio signalling. (D.C.Pearce)

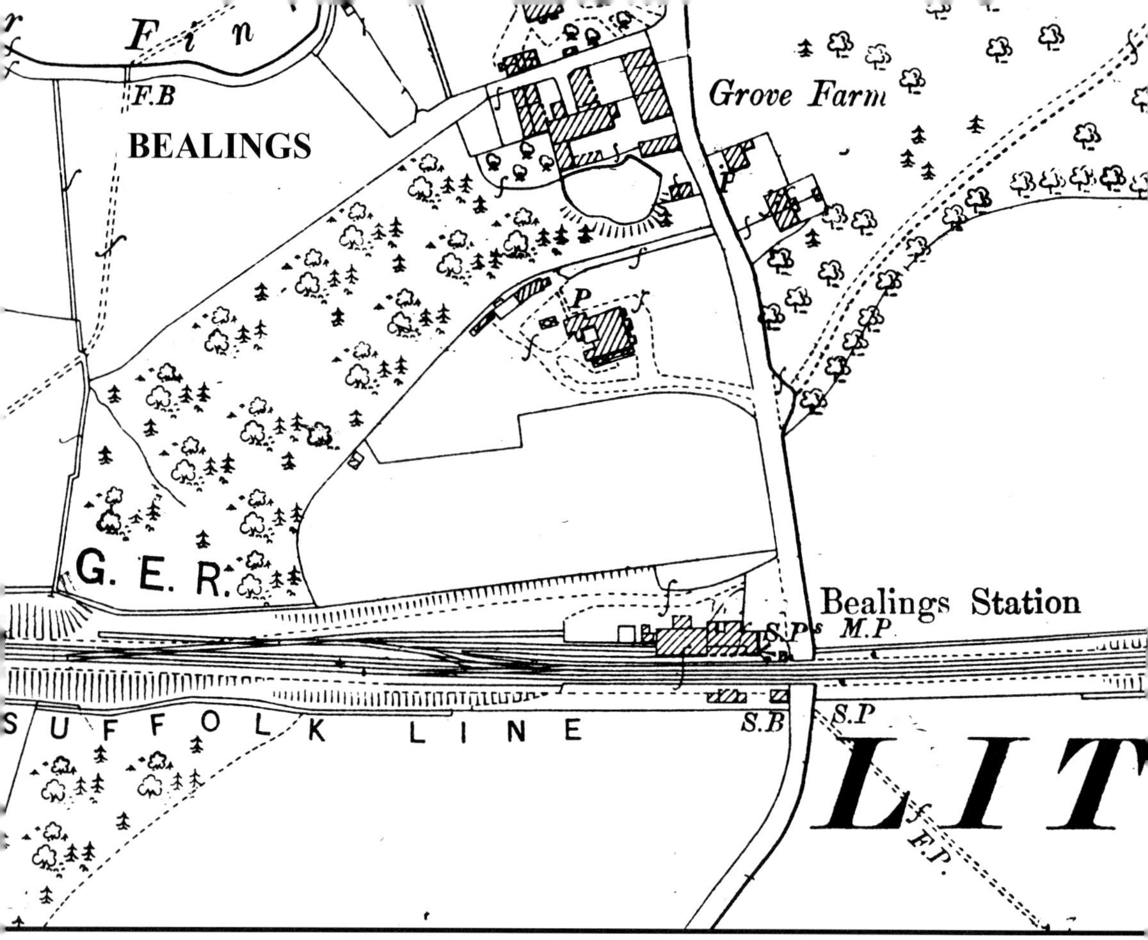

The basic features of a small country station are illustrated in this 1904 plan, showing as it does a goods shed, an end loading dock and a general purpose yard area, in addition to the passenger facilities. The station was closed to passengers on 17th September 1956, although freight services continued until 19th April 1965.

29. We are looking east along the up platform at Bealings on a summer day in the late 1920s. The painted station name board on this platform contrasts with its enamel Great Eastern counterpart on the other side. (Stations UK)

30. An unusual "train" of three engines makes its way through the station in 1955. As a bonus, we have a rare glimpse inside the goods shed, through which so much of the produce of the community passed over the years. (Stations UK)

31. Class B17 4-6-0 no.61665 *Leicester City* heads the up milk train over the level crossing shortly before closure. Even at this time, the station flowerbeds are well tended, and the GER nameboard remains in place on the goods shed wall. (EADT)

32. The buildings were intact on 31st July 1961, some five years after the passenger closure, although the goods shed entrance had been bricked up, and the platform edging had been removed. Strangely, nobody had bothered to remove the lamp posts! (J.Watling)

33. The signal box continued to control the level crossing for many years after the station closed. Smoke drifting from the chimney shows that the signalman is keeping warm as a class 105 DMU speeds north through the snow. (I.Cowley)

34. The old order was eventually swept away in 1984. The new style level crossing was photographed on 10th April - no time had been wasted in demolishing the redundant signal box. (R.J.Adderson)

35. Class 37 no.37050 speeds north over the crossing with the 17.00 from Liverpool Street to Lowestoft on 5th May 1984. A week later, through trains to and from London would run for the last time. (H.N.James/J.Day)

EAST OF BEALINGS

36. The scenic nature of this stretch of line is emphasised by this picture of a class 105 DMU heading northwards near the village of Martlesham on a May evening in 1984. (I.Cowley)

37. This three arch viaduct, spanning a deep wooded cutting, is a prominent feature of the line hereabouts. A class 47 leans to the curve through the centre arch of the viaduct with a down express in the 1980s. (I.Cowley)

38. With Martlesham Creek in the background, a class 153 heads towards Ipswich on 14th July 1999. (G.L.Kenworthy)

39. No. 37059 winds its way through the wooded countryside south of Woodbridge with a "Saturdays Only" train from Lowestoft to Liverpool Street on 4th September 1982. Contrary to popular opinion, rural East Anglia is rarely flat and featureless. (I.Cowley)

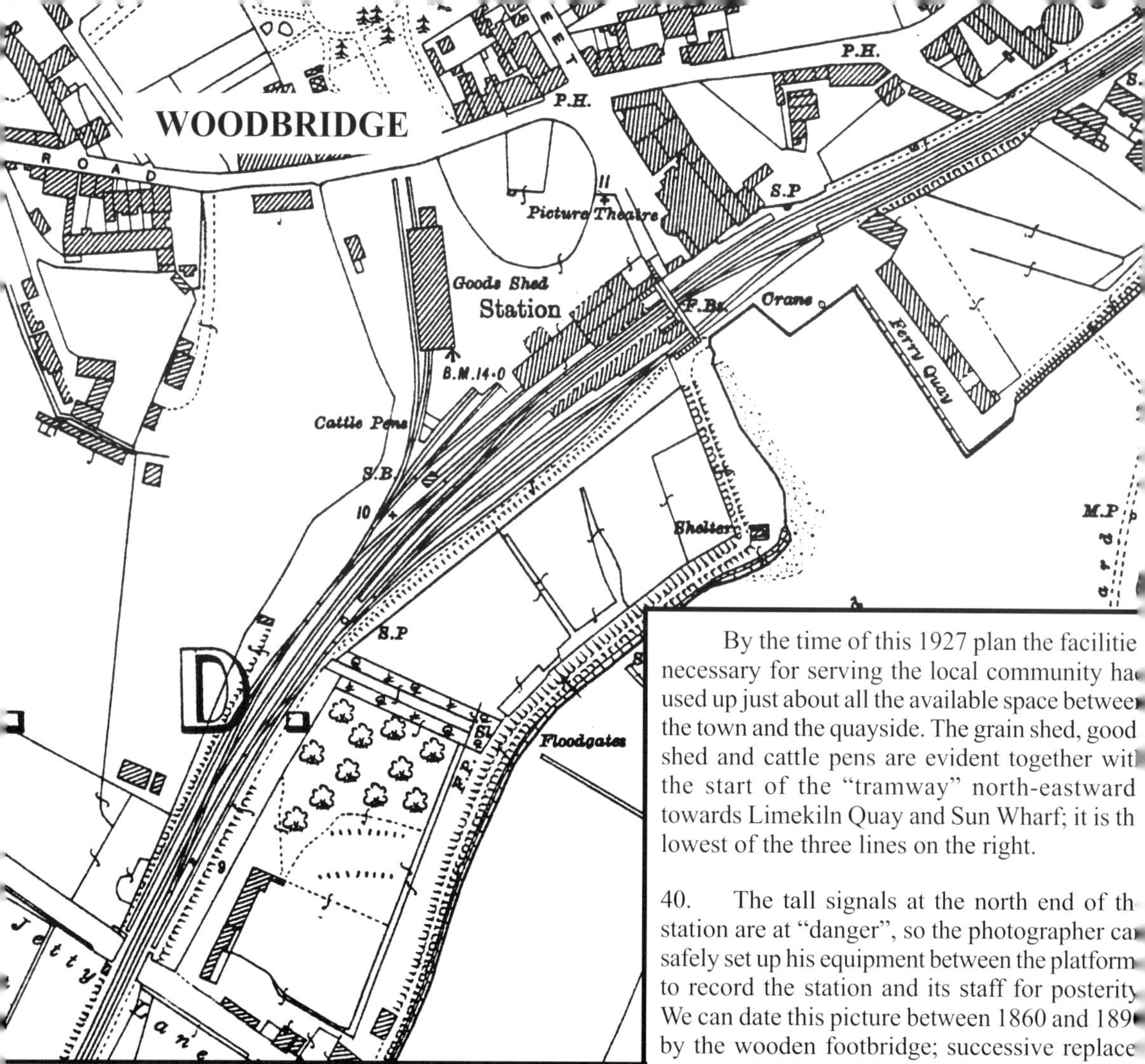

By the time of this 1927 plan the facilitie necessary for serving the local community ha used up just about all the available space betwee the town and the quayside. The grain shed, good shed and cattle pens are evident together wit the start of the "tramway" north-eastward towards Limekiln Quay and Sun Wharf; it is th lowest of the three lines on the right.

40. The tall signals at the north end of th station are at "danger", so the photographer ca safely set up his equipment between the platform to record the station and its staff for posterity We can date this picture between 1860 and 189 by the wooden footbridge; successive replace ment footbridges will be seen in pictures nos. 4 and 49. (L.Cooper collection)

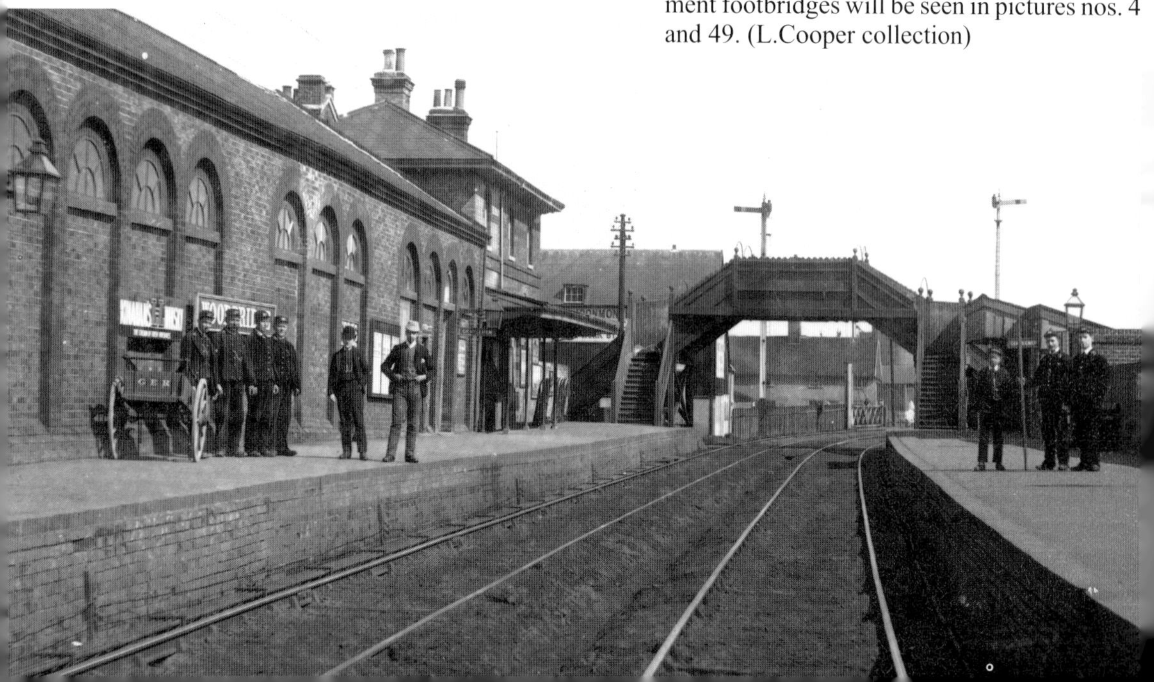

41. Passengers make their way along the station approach road as a GER 2-4-0 stands at the platform. The station is close to the waterfront, and the schooner *English Rose* moored at the quay in the background completes an interesting combination of rail and water transport in Victorian Suffolk. (Suffolk Record Office Ipswich SPS 593)

42. This panorama of the curved approach to the station from the south illustrates clearly how big an area the railway covered in 1911. Facilities for freight traffic were extensive, and a line of wagons can be seen outside the substantial grain shed, which is at virtually right angles to the running lines. (HMRS)

43. Another view of the station taken on the same day shows a wagon in the goods shed, adjacent to the platform. We can only pay tribute to the dedication – some would say courage - of the early photographer who clambered to the top of lofty signal posts with a heavy plate camera to record these scenes. (HMRS)

45. Class J15 0-6-0 no. 65467 has finished shunting and passes a vintage GER ground signal as it heads north through the station with the pick-up goods for the Snape and Framlingham branches on 10th October 1956. (R.C.Riley)

44. We complete this set of 1911 pictures with a view northwards from the station, this time taken from the more solid vantage point of the public footbridge. The line on the right is the tramway, a long siding some 41 chains long, which served riverside industries. Operated by horses to the end, it remained in use until the late 1950s. (HMRS)

WOODBRIDGE

←

46. Horses were used to shunt wagons in the yard, as well as on the tramway, until the late 1950s. By then, Woodbridge was one of the few places on British Railways where this once commonplace practice could be seen. (EADT)

48. The ancient tide mill, a well-known feature of the town, can be seen in the distance to the right of the loco as class B12 4-6-0 no.61577 heads south from the station with a passenger train on 28th July 1958. (R.W.Smith)

←

47. Class D16/3 4-4-0 no. 62546 *Claud Hamilton*, the second locomotive to bear this distinguished name, accelerates away from the Woodbridge stop with a morning local train on 10th October 1956. The driver, guard, and one of the passengers are leaning out, enjoying a heady mix of steam and autumn sunshine, with perhaps a whiff of sea air from the nearby Deben estuary. (R.C.Riley)

49. A view northwards around 1960 shows that the goods shed has been demolished, although many features of both the railway and the town have changed little in some 50 years. (NRS Archive)

50. The River Deben and the railway converge to the south of Woodbridge and run roughly parallel as far as Wickham Market. The tide is out as no. 37140 runs into the station with the 10.30 "Saturdays Only" train from Lowestoft to Liverpool Street on 11th September 1982. (I.Cowley)

51. Providing a foretaste of things to come, the prototype "Sprinter" unit no. 150001 runs over the crossings at the north end of the station whilst working the 09.02 from Lowestoft on 9th November 1985. The gatekeeper at the further crossing has wasted no time in opening the gates to road traffic behind the train. (I.Cowley)

52. Although the town continues to generate worthwhile passenger traffic, the platforms are rarely as crowded as they were on 3rd July 1988, when 37144 arrived with a railtour. (I.Cowley)

53. The station buildings survived all the changes, and in 1999 housed a restaurant, taxi firm and Tourist Information Centre. Again we see signs in connection with the radio signalling, as no. 153306 pauses briefly on its way north as the 10.50 from Ipswich on 11th May that year. A visit from the weedkiller train would seem to be overdue. (R.J.Adderson)

NORTH OF WOODBRIDGE

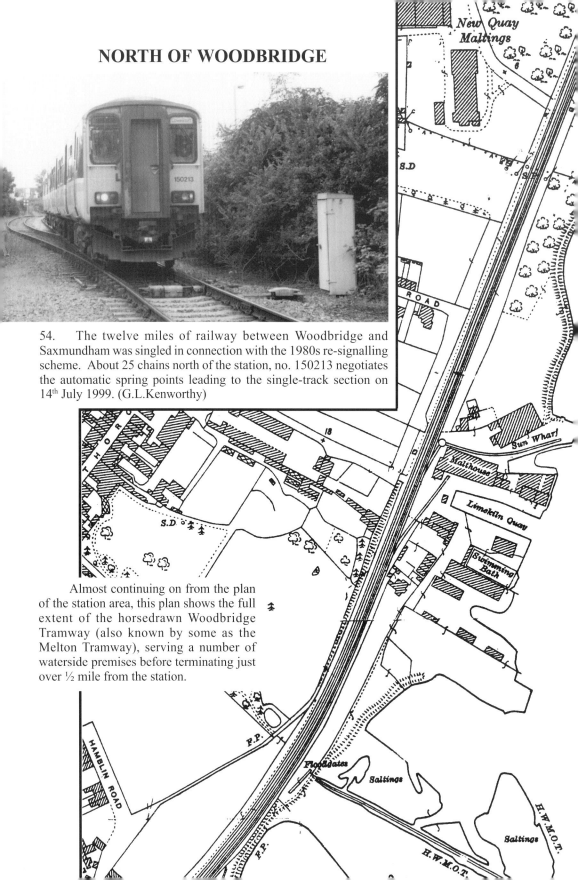

54. The twelve miles of railway between Woodbridge and Saxmundham was singled in connection with the 1980s re-signalling scheme. About 25 chains north of the station, no. 150213 negotiates the automatic spring points leading to the single-track section on 14th July 1999. (G.L.Kenworthy)

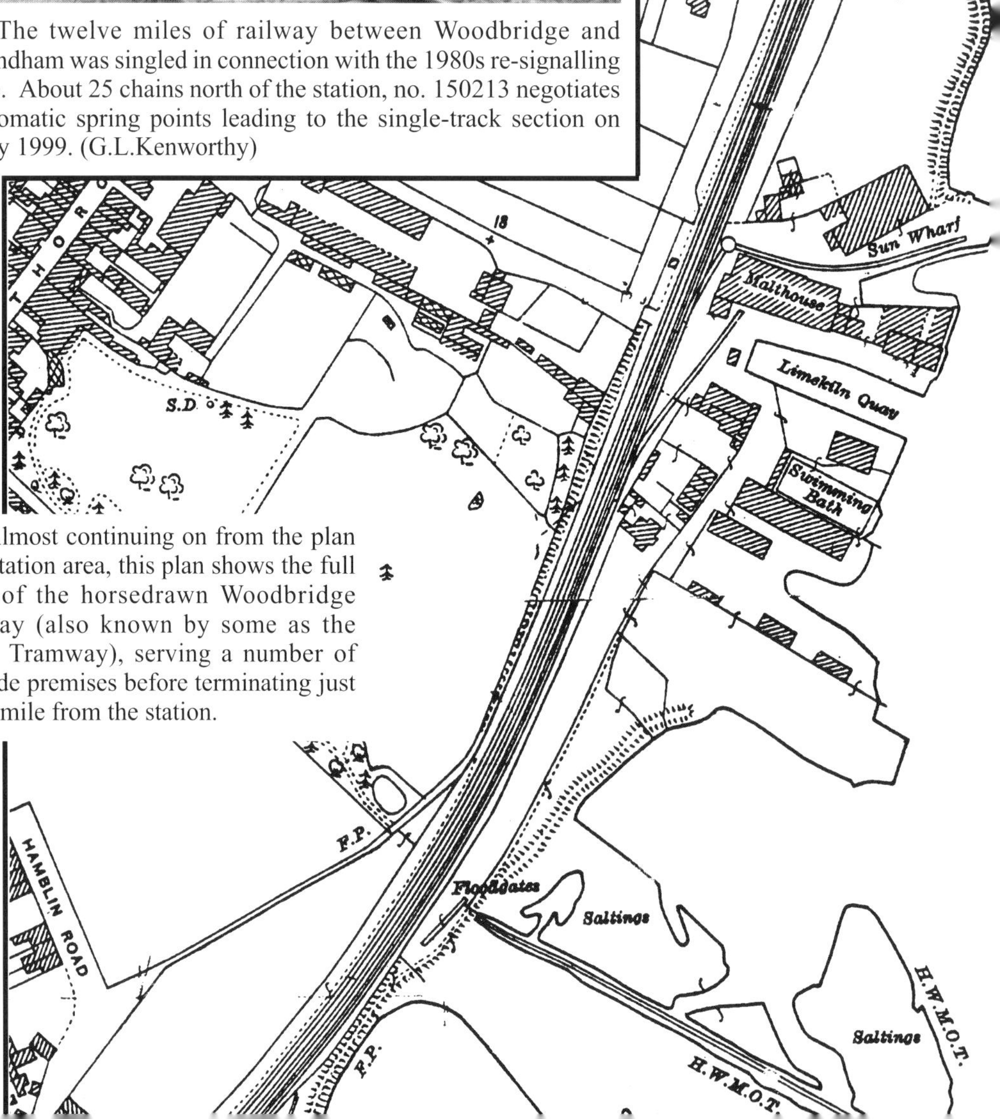

Almost continuing on from the plan of the station area, this plan shows the full extent of the horsedrawn Woodbridge Tramway (also known by some as the Melton Tramway), serving a number of waterside premises before terminating just over ½ mile from the station.

55. Despite the switchback nature of the route, there were some sixty level crossings between Westerfield and Saxmundham alone. Admittedly, many of these were unstaffed occupation or footpath crossings, but nonetheless they represented a severe drain on the finances of the line. These two crossings serving Limekiln Quay and Sun Wharf, seen here on 14th July 1999, were amongst those automated during the mid 1980s. (G.L.Kenworthy)

56. As the 12.47 train from Ipswich makes its way towards Melton on a grass-grown single track, a speed restriction sign warns the driver not to exceed 55 mph. In July 1999 it was difficult to visualise that this had once been a double track main line with considerable commercial activity to the right of the train. (R.J.Adderson)

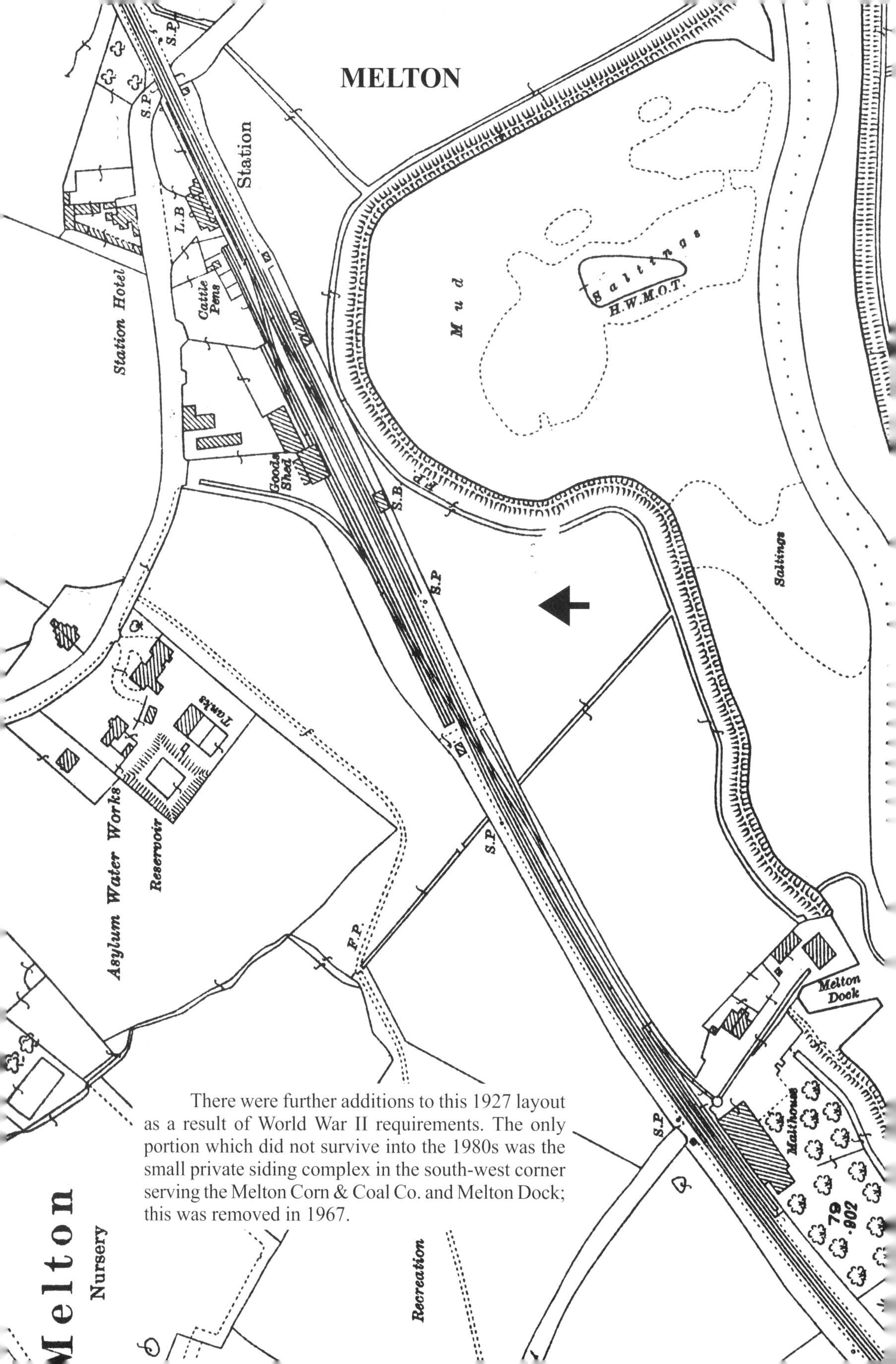

There were further additions to this 1927 layout as a result of World War II requirements. The only portion which did not survive into the 1980s was the small private siding complex in the south-west corner serving the Melton Corn & Coal Co. and Melton Dock; this was removed in 1967.

57. This was the scene looking south along the down platform at Melton on a summer day in 1928. Beyond the boarded crossing connecting the staggered platforms, a class J15 0-6-0 busies itself by the goods shed. (Stations UK)

58. The driver of the J15 looks back as he propels some wagons back into the goods yard on the same day. This time we are looking north from the up platform. (Stations UK)

59. Class B17 4-6-0 no. 61637 *Thorpe Hall* arrives with a down stopping train, shortly before the station was closed to passengers on 2nd May 1955. The porter looks on, perhaps pondering on an uncertain future. (EADT)

60. Some five years after the passenger closure, little had changed. Although the waiting room on the up platform and the goods shed had gone, the main station building was still inhabited, as the television aerial testifies. (NRS Archive)

61. During 1972 the goods yard was used to unload stone trains from the Western Region, and a Ruston & Hornsby diesel mechanical locomotive was sent to assist with shunting. On 16th August, the little diesel was dwarfed by a row of hoppers as no. 5683 propelled a loaded train into the yard. The coal merchant's lorry is a reminder of more traditional traffic. (R.J.Adderson)

62. Despite the withdrawal of passenger services, the track layout remained surprisingly complete. As late as June 1984, the diagram in the signal box showed a complex system of points and sidings. (R.J.Adderson)

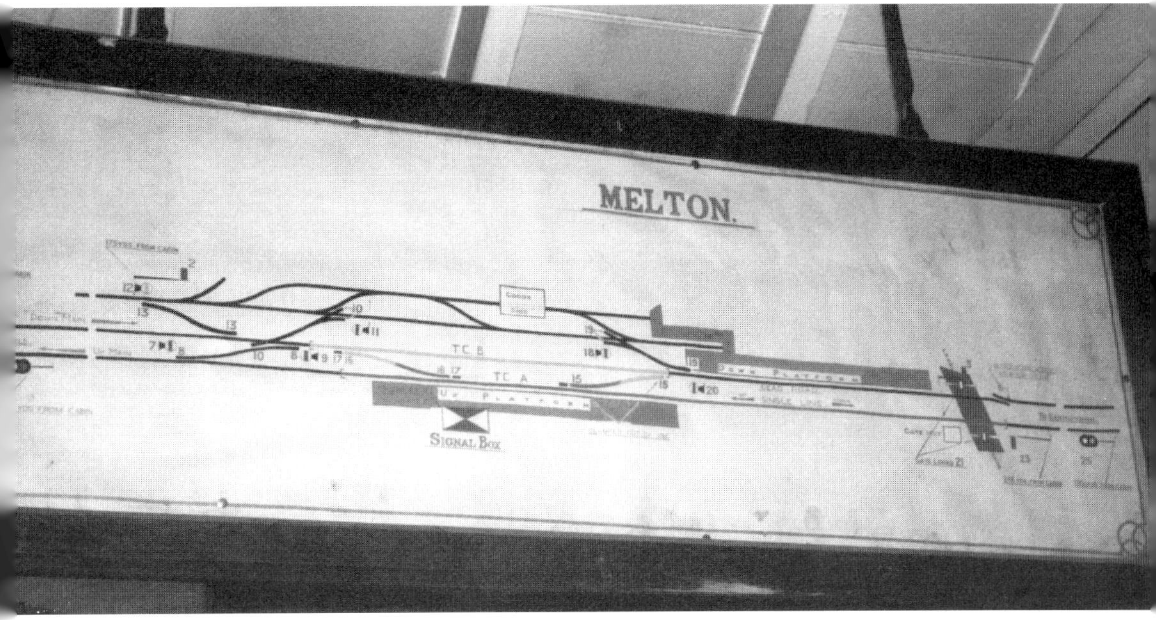

63. Coal traffic continued until 1984, and no.31107 is seen here on arrival with the twice-weekly working on 9th December 1983. By this time such a train had become an extremely rare sight on the British Rail system, as indeed had the shunter with his pole. (I.Cowley)

64. For some time before the radio-signalling scheme came into operation, all trains ran over the former up line between Melton and Saxmundham. A train for Lowestoft is seen on 23rd June 1984 negotiating the new facing crossover which was installed in connection with this movement, while the signalman waits to hand over the token for the single line northwards. (R.J.Adderson)

65. The 09.53 train from Ipswich is the centre of attention at the official reopening of the station on 5th September 1984. The first train had called two days previously, but the ceremony was delayed until after the school holidays, thus enabling local children to participate in the event. (I.Cowley)

66. There are no "customers" waiting for the 13.12 to Lowestoft as no. 150257 draws to a halt on 11th May 1999. At the time the station building was housing a butcher's shop, but had changed little externally over the years. However, a comparison with picture 60 will reveal that the platform had been shortened before the station was reopened. (R.J.Adderson)

WICKHAM MARKET

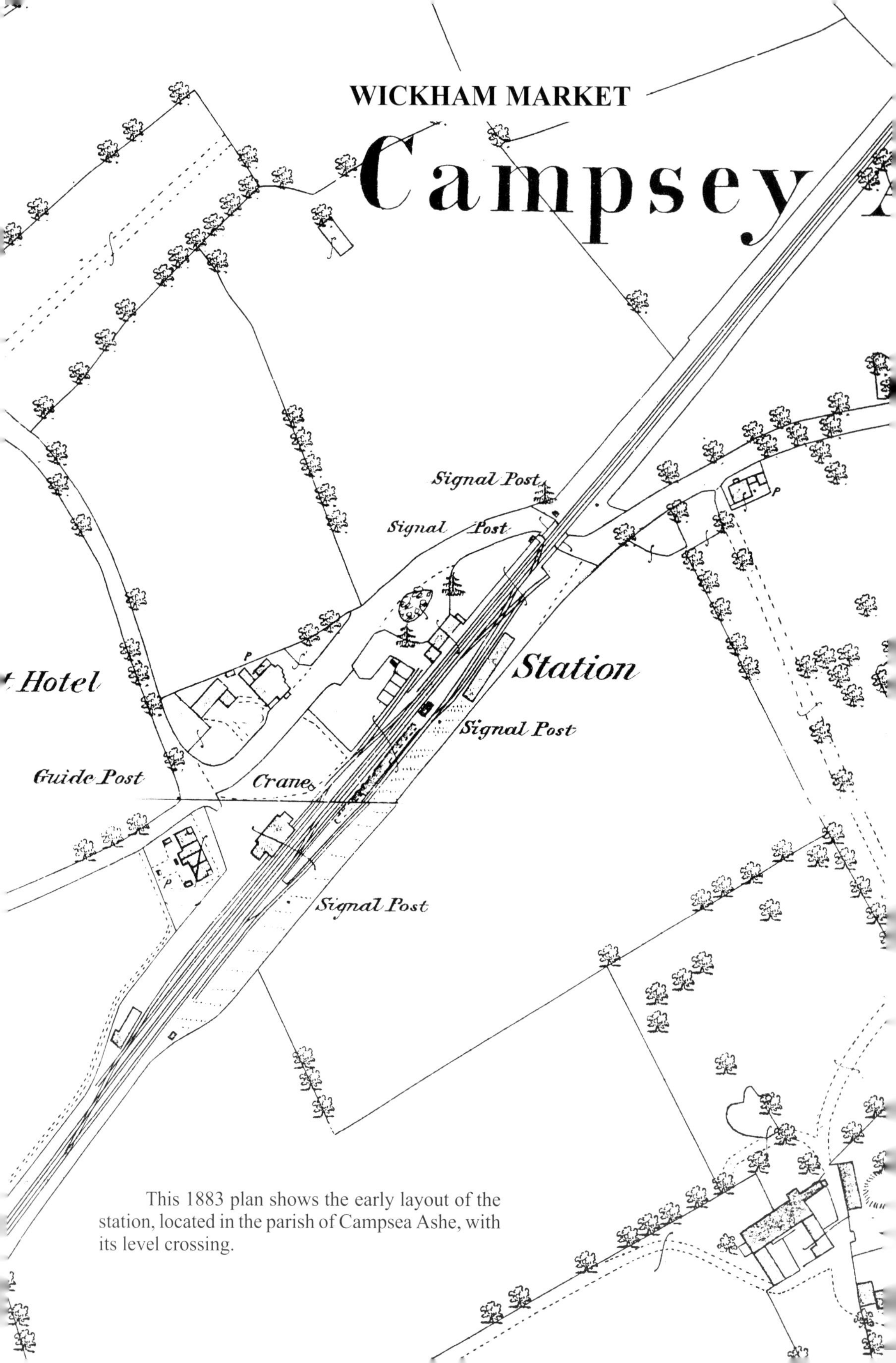

This 1883 plan shows the early layout of the station, located in the parish of Campsea Ashe, with its level crossing.

This 1904 plan post-dates the elimination of the level crossing and the building of a replacement bridge. About 300 yards north of the station there was, at this time, a short siding, capable of taking no more than about three wagons. It is thought that this may have been used as access to a small area owned by the GER to load the fill required for constructing the road approaches to the new bridge.

67. This early photograph looking northwards along the platform shows the level crossing, which was replaced by a bridge over the railway during 1902. (Suffolk Record Office Ipswich SPS 1328)

68. The level crossing and lofty GER signals feature again here. The station appears to be well endowed with porters' trolleys, and there is a bookstall at right angles to the track in the centre of the picture. (Suffolk Record Office Ipswich SPS 1327)

69. The replacement road bridge is a feature of this 1911 scene. We can see that substantial, expensive earthworks have been necessary to carry the road over the railway. (HMRS)

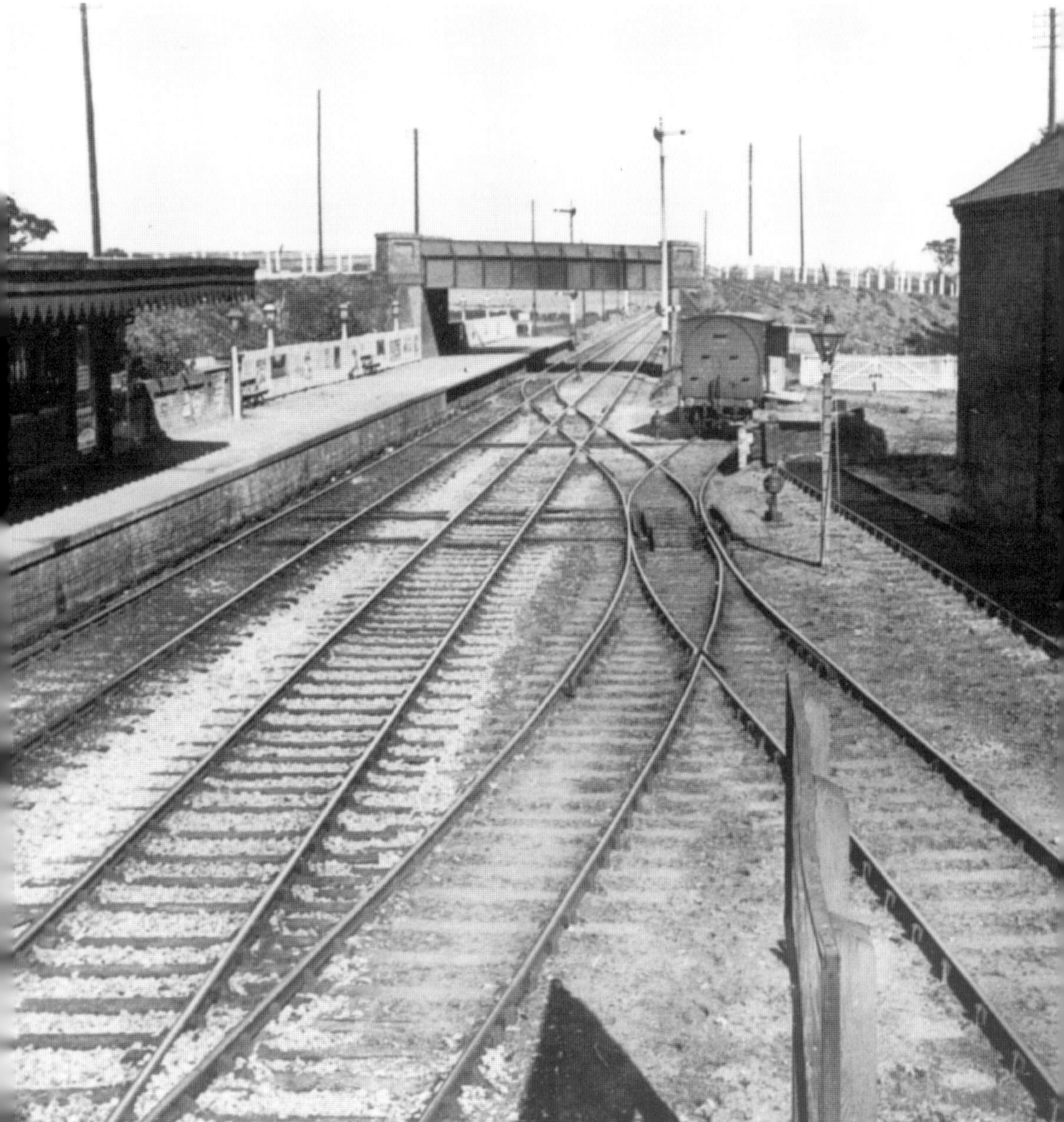

70. This view southwards from the road bridge shows the change in the platform facing at the spot from which the platform had been extended north over the old level crossing. It is hardly likely that delays to road traffic in this rural area would have led to replacement of the crossing, so the bridge was almost certainly built in connection with the platform extension. However, as we shall see, roads bisecting platforms on the level were not a problem elsewhere on the East Suffolk line. (HMRS)

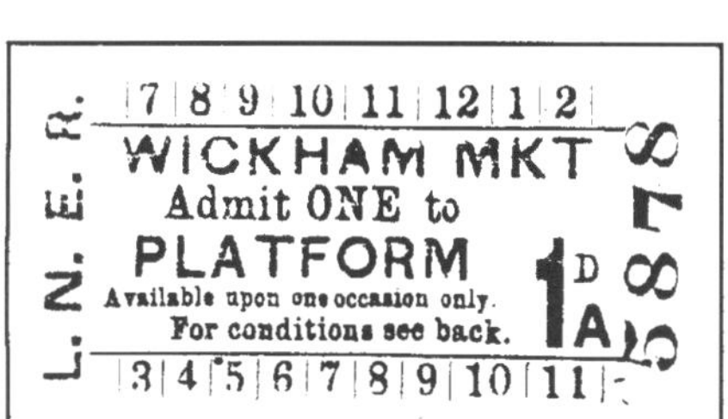

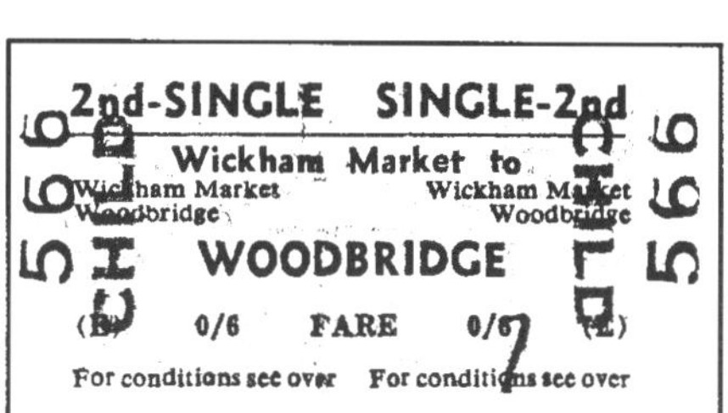

71. This was the signalman's view across the goods yard in 1911. The Consolidated Petroleum Company depot in the yard was an early victim of road transport. (HMRS)

72. The coaches of the Framlingham train stand at the outer face of the peculiarly shaped up island platform in the early 1950s. A few goods wagons are dotted around, but there is no sign of life, even though a down train is standing at the platform. (Stations UK)

73. Services on the Framlingham line were far from intensive, and the branch train would spend long hours hanging around at either end of its journey. On this occasion it has ventured into the goods shed to pick up a few wagons prior to the next amble down the branch. (H.Moffatt)

→

74. A low winter sun illuminates the station on 6th December 1959. Following the withdrawal of the branch passenger services, the outer face of the island platform had been fenced off. (NRS Archive)

→

75. The railwayman is trying to attract somebody's attention as a Metro Cammell DMU approaches the up platform on 1st December 1962. In the short siding, three cattle wagons provide a reminder of what was once an intensive traffic in this farming region. The signal box was abolished from 19th July 1965, leaving the former Junction signalbox to control trains in the area until March 1971.(E.Wilmshurst)

WICKHAM MARKET

76. The yard crane was a long-lived feature of the goods yard. We have seen it in a picture from 1911, and this close up was taken some fifty years later, on 31st July 1961. It had originally been built as a travelling crane, and the design of the bearings suggests that it could have dated back to the 1850s. It was listed in 1938 as having a 6-ton capacity.(J.Watling)

77. Whilst the down line was being upgraded in 1984, all trains used the former up line. A single passenger has left the train and makes her way off the station as her train continues its journey northwards on 10th April. The blue enamel running-in board was a rare survivor of its type by this time. (R.J.Adderson)

78. Forming the 13.09 train from Lowestoft, no. 153306 runs into the station on 11th May 1999. It is now very much a "basic railway", but the goods shed and station building survive as reminders of busier days. (R.J.Adderson)

NORTH OF WICKHAM MARKET

79. Looking north from the road bridge, we see the 07.15 train from Lowestoft slowing for the station stop on 14th May 1984. Behind the class 101 railcars, the boundary fence is set back from the line, providing a visual reminder of the siding mentioned in the 1904 map caption. Round the curve towards the junction, a brake van stands on the down line, which is being relaid with continuously welded track. (I.Cowley)

WICKHAM MARKET JUNCTION

The simplest form of junction from a double track main line to a single line branch is illustrated in this 1904 plan.

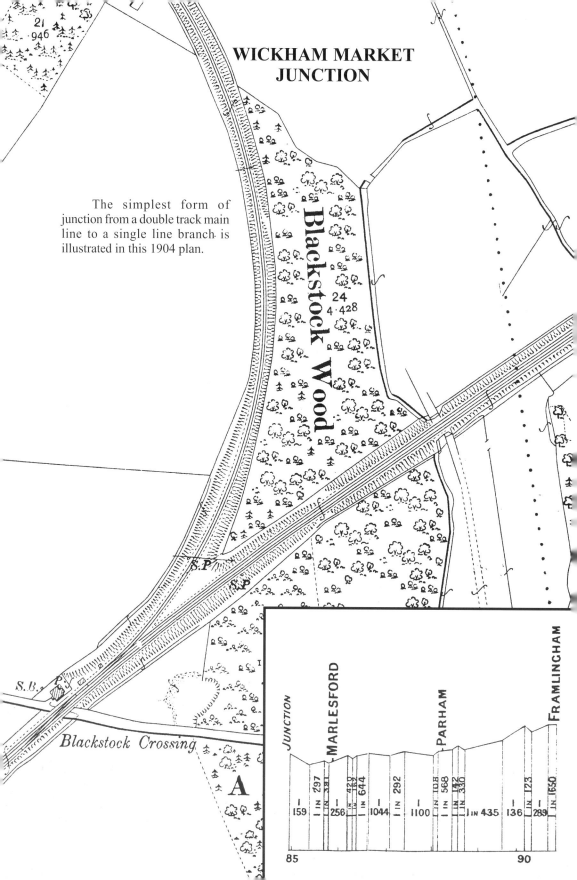

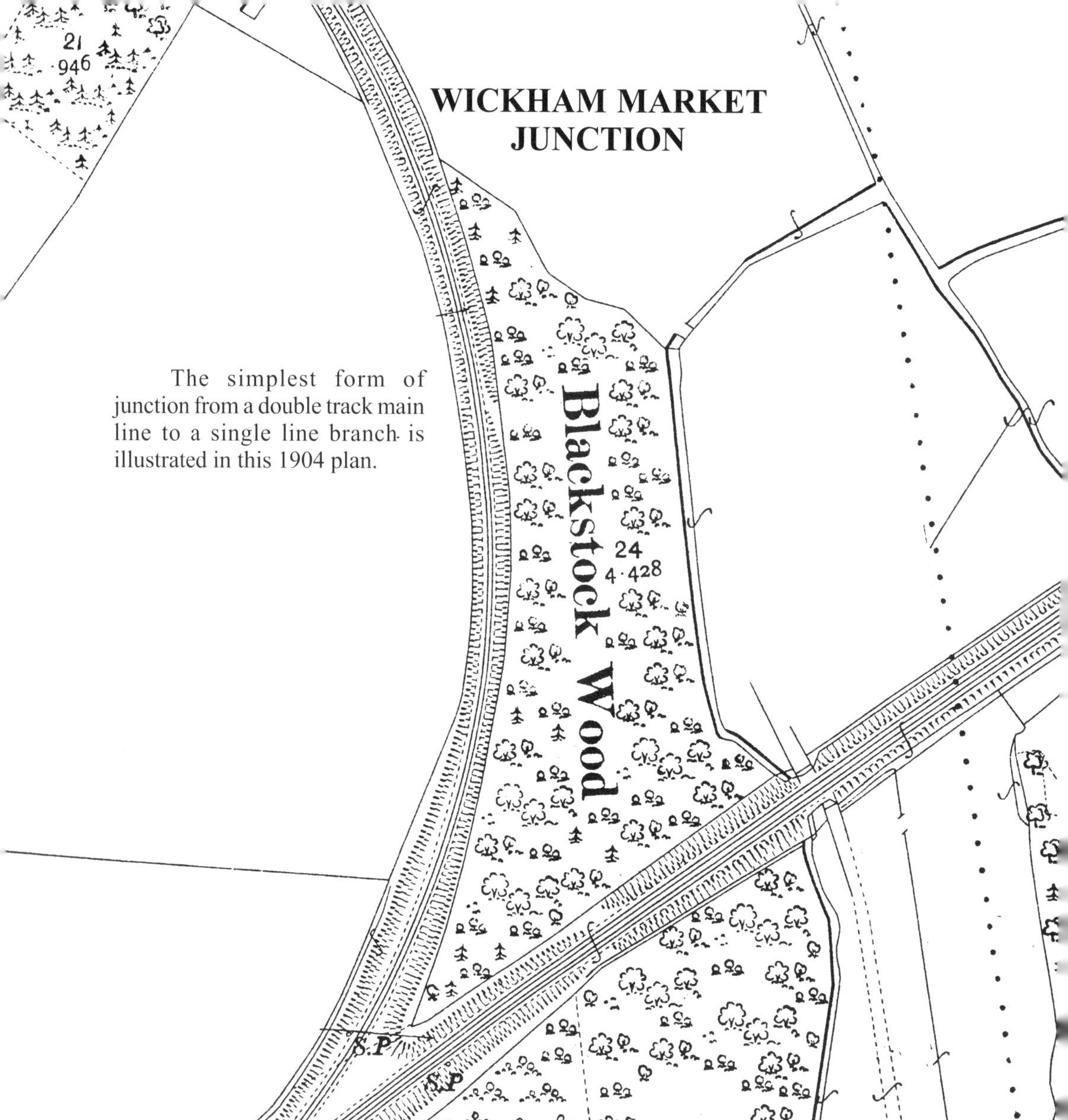

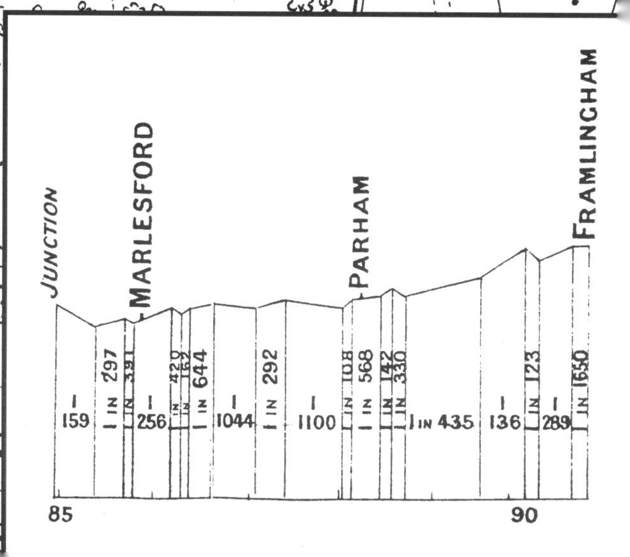

80. Trains for Framlingham ran down the main line for some ¾ mile, before heading north-westwards at Wickham Market junction. Looking north over the level crossing around 1960 we see the branch curving away from the main line beyond the signal box. (NRS Archive)

81. After being held at the junction signal, class J15 0-6-0 no. 65389 comes off the branch with the goods from Framlingham on 19th February 1960. (NRS Archive)

82. The driver of no. D5045 looks back as the branch goods negotiates the crossover to the main line in April 1965. By the brake van, the signalman takes in the scene from the veranda of his box – he knows that he will have few opportunities to savour it in the future, as total closure of the branch is imminent. (H.N.James/J.Day)

2. Framlingham Branch

MARLESFORD

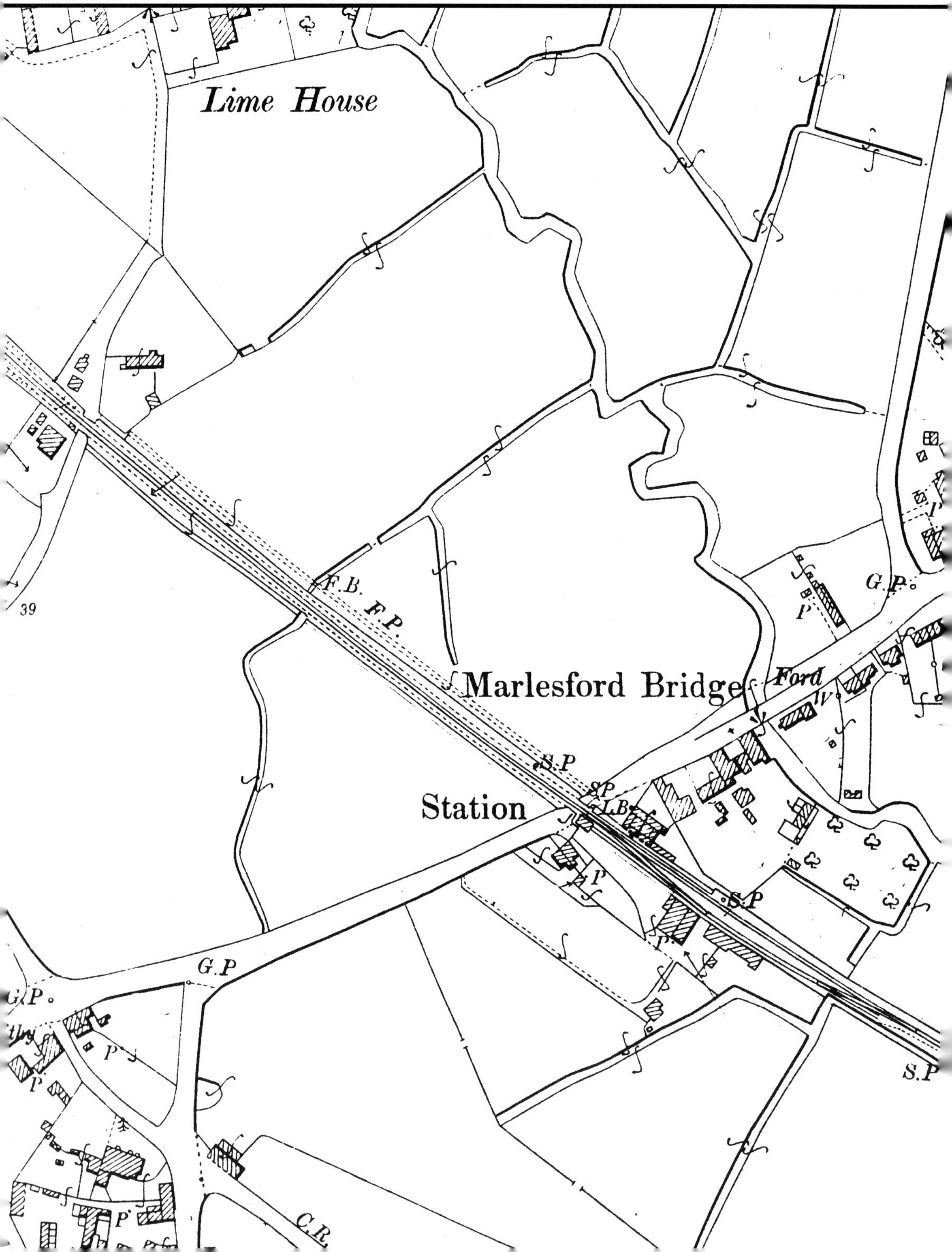

83. This view of Marlesford station in Great Eastern days shows the signal box and the level crossing over what would later become the A12 trunk road. The coach body on the platform is that of GER suburban brake no. 297, built in 1874, which was moved here to provide additional covered storage accommodation following its withdrawal in late 1901. (Lens of Sutton)

← Although a further siding was later installed behind the platform, the modest extent of the station siding facilities in this 1904 plan make an interesting contrast with the impressive appearance of the station buildings seen in the photographs.

84. The south-western aspect of the station was a familiar sight to travellers on the A12 road. By the time this picture was taken, passenger trains no longer ran, although everything is still very tidy. (Stations UK)

85. With the base of the signal box in the foreground, a class J15 runs through the station with a substantial goods train. This picture dates from the 1950s, when the Framlingham goods train also served the Aldeburgh branch, and the amount of coal piled high on the tender indicates that the crew is anticipating a long day! (K.A.Leighton)

86. Returning from Framlingham, class J15 0-6-0 no. 65389 pulls into the station on 4th May 1958. The old coach body is still there, and it was destined to survive long after the tracks had been removed. (R.C.Riley)

87. A few minutes later, the fireman was operating the point lever as no. 65389 shunted briskly at the east end of the station. This train was always smartly operated, being a bonus working – the sooner the crew got back to Ipswich, the more they were paid. On this occasion, however, there was an even greater incentive, for it was Cup Final Saturday, and the prospect of Bolton v Manchester United on the radio, or possibly on a flickering black and white television, beckoned! (R.C.Riley)

88. A short goods train from Framlingham runs through the unspoilt Suffolk countryside as it passes Ford level crossing, near Marlesford, behind class J15 0-6-0 no. 65472 on 19th September 1959. (R.W.Smith)

HACHESTON HALT

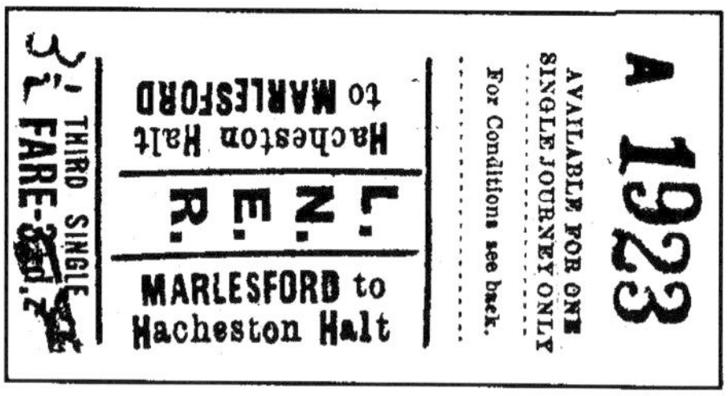

89. A single photograph tells all there is to tell about Hacheston Halt….a lamp, a trespassers sign and a battered nameboard overlooking a short rail-level "platform", at the end of an insignificant country lane; it opened in 1924. The regular branch train was equipped with retractable steps for the use of the halt's occasional passenger. "Passengers to and from Hacheston Halt must join, or alight from, the special car provided" announced the timetable. (Stations UK)

PARHAM

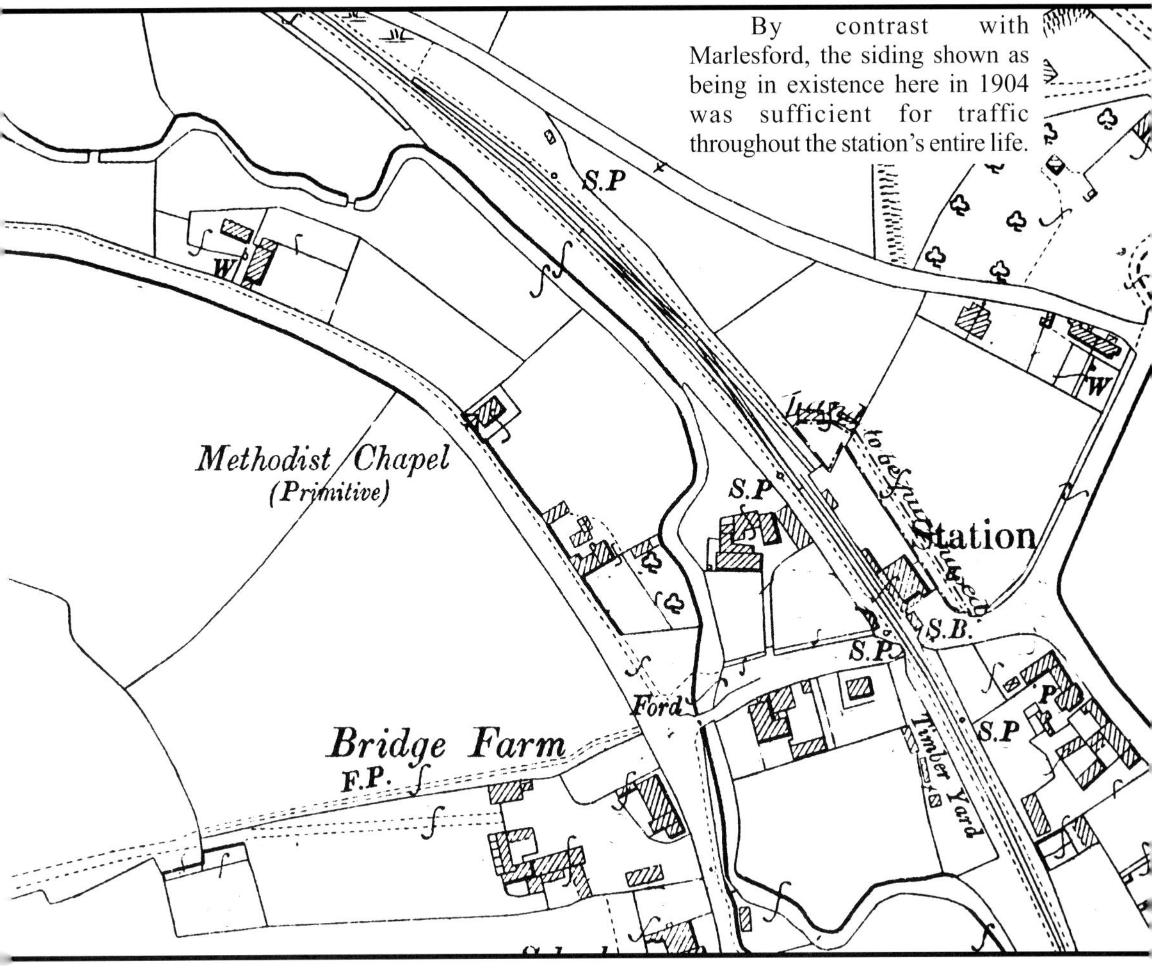

By contrast with Marlesford, the siding shown as being in existence here in 1904 was sufficient for traffic throughout the station's entire life.

90. No doubt fascinated by his presence, the children of the village gather by the river bridge to watch the photographer as he records the scene north-eastwards to the station. (Stations UK)

91. Looking south-eastwards, the signal box, level crossing and signals all contribute to a compact picture of a country station in the early years of the twentieth century.
(Suffolk Record Office Ipswich SPS1337)

92. The signal box was abolished in the mid 1920s, long before the passenger services ceased. In later days, access to the yard was controlled by means of the ground frame in the foreground of this picture. (Stations UK)

93. In the distance the train from Framlingham rounds the curve towards the platform. The presence of two photographers, as well as what appears to be bunting suspended from the awning, suggests this picture may have been taken on the last day of the passenger service, 3rd November 1952. (Stations UK)

94. Beyond the crossing gates, the station slumbers in the winter sunshine on 6th December 1959. By now, only an occasional goods train would disturb this peaceful scene. The station building still appears to be in good condition, and was subsequently converted to a private house.(NRS Archive)

95. Returning to the junction on an April day in 1965, no. D5045 and half-a-dozen wagons rattle past the ancient church of St Mary the Virgin at Parham. (H.N.James/J.Day)

FRAMLINGHAM

All the facilities to be expected at a branch terminus serving a small, but reasonably prosperous, market town can be seen in this 1904 plan. There is an engine shed at the southern end of the area, to the west of the line; a granary almost opposite the signal box (S.B.); a large goods shed a little further north and a crane of 5-ton capacity. On the west side of the station buildings are cattle pens and a loading dock, while the siding along the eastern boundary serves a range of coal sheds and another granary. The site is completed by a range of staff accommodation along Station Terrace and the Station Hotel, in the north-east corner.

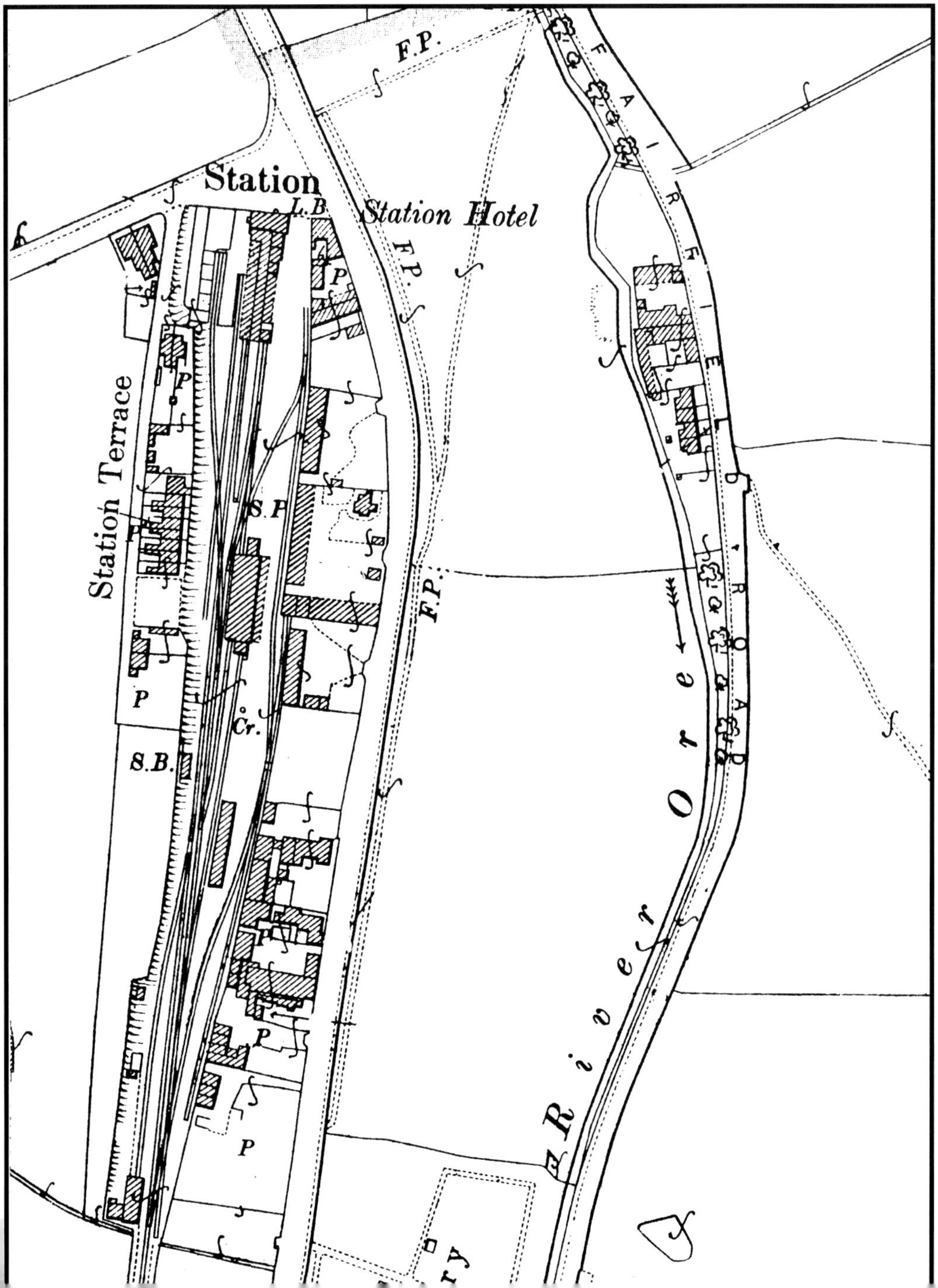

96. The station was a solid two-storey building, and is seen here in the early years of the twentieth century. As at so many places, the Station Hotel was conveniently situated for thirsty travellers. (Lens of Sutton)

97. The single platform was sufficient for the short and infrequent passenger trains that were provided to serve a population of around 2500. (Stations UK)

98. Mixed trains were a feature of the branch. On this occasion, there were no wagons for the up train, but the brake van next to the engine suggests that there will be some on the return from the junction. Class F6 2-4-2T no.67230 waits for departure time in the early 1950s. (H.N.James/J.Day)

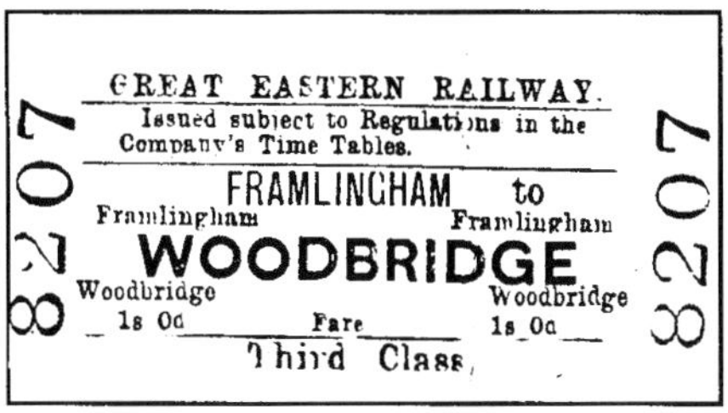

99. No. 67230 was allocated to Ipswich shed for many years and was a regular performer on the branch. Here it is again, passing the goods shed as it leaves with two main line coaches forming the 3.20 pm to Wickham Market on 2nd June 1952. The vehicle by the goods shed appears to be the runner wagon for a rail mounted goods crane. (R.K.Blencowe)

→

100. For some years after the passenger closure, special trains were run at the start and end of term for students at Framlingham College, although members of the general public were allowed to travel on them. Class B12 4-6-0 no. 61561 backs out of the station, having worked the last such train on 3rd May 1958. The photographer had travelled down from London and recalls being treated with a mixture of respect and suspicion by the schoolboys on the train, as they thought he might be a new master! (R.C.Riley)

101. Class J15 0-6-0 no. 65389 busies itself in the sidings on 4th May 1958, a fine spring morning. The signal box, although externally intact, has been reduced to a ground frame. (R.C.Riley)

102. The platform awnings, redundant for some seven years, are still in place on 6th December 1959. By now, the track is beginning to look neglected. (NRS Archive)

103. D5048 waits with the branch goods on 1st December 1962. Its train is made up of a mixture of coal wagons, box vans and grain hoppers, proving that the branch handled a variety of traffic even at this late date. (E.Wilmshurst)

104. Although diesel locomotives were used on the branch goods in its final years, the visit o D5595 with a special passenger train on 12th April 1963 was probably unique. The train is at leas four coaches too long for the platform. (A.E.Bennett)

105. The line was lifted soon after the last goods train ran, as this picture, taken on 14th Augus 1965, testifies. Without ceremony, the railway had left Framlingham after serving the town for jus over a century, leaving just a few piles of sleepers and some rusty rails to mark its passing. (J.Watling)

3. Snape Junction to Saxmundham

SNAPE JUNCTION

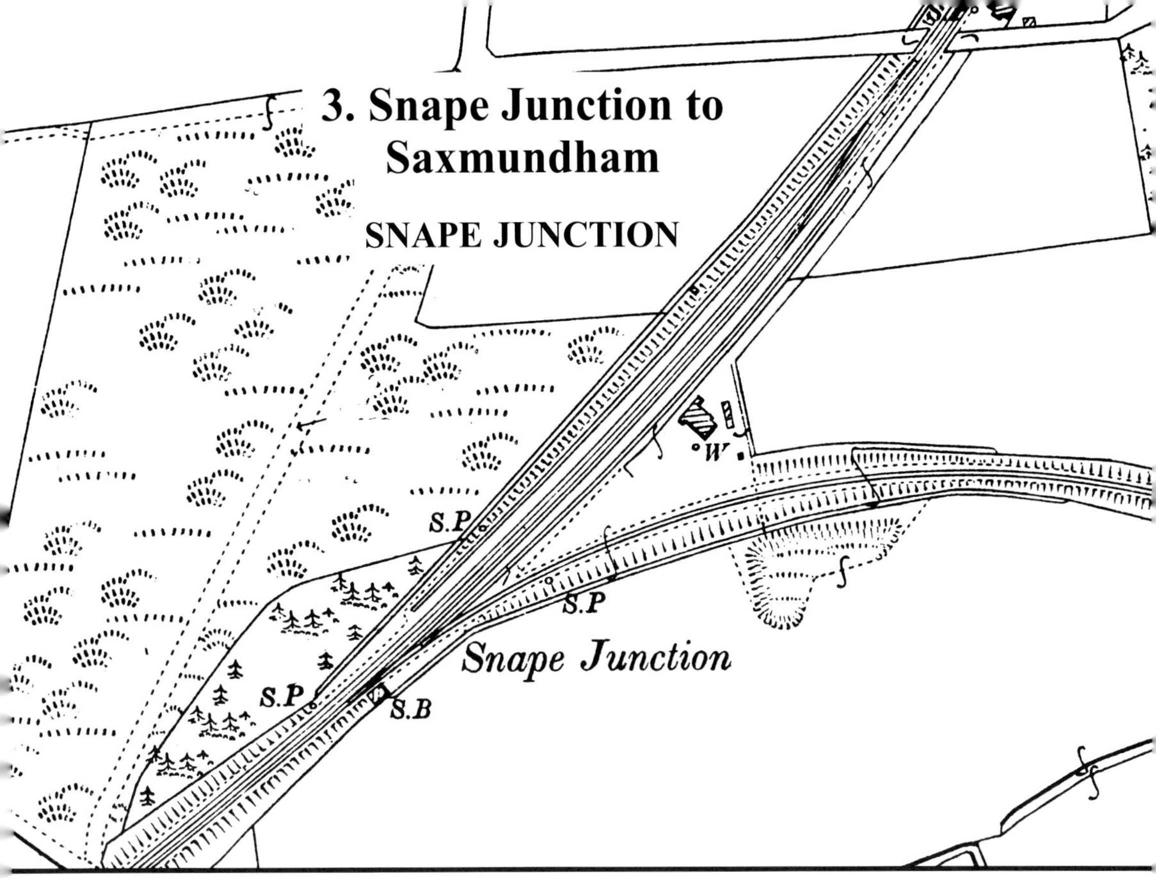

Compared with the stark simplicity of Wickham Market Junction, albeit within a short distance of Wickham Market station itself, this location at the start of a branch of less than 1½ miles fairly bristles with siding accommodation in this 1904 plan. Although the branch closed in March 1960, the signal box continued to function as a block post for a further nine months or so.

106. We now return to the main line for the last few miles of our journey to Saxmundham. The layout at Snape Junction is clearly illustrated in this view looking north-east from the signal box on 30th September 1956. To the right, the presence of a railtour on the Snape branch provides unprecedented human activity at this remote and usually lonely location. (Stations UK)

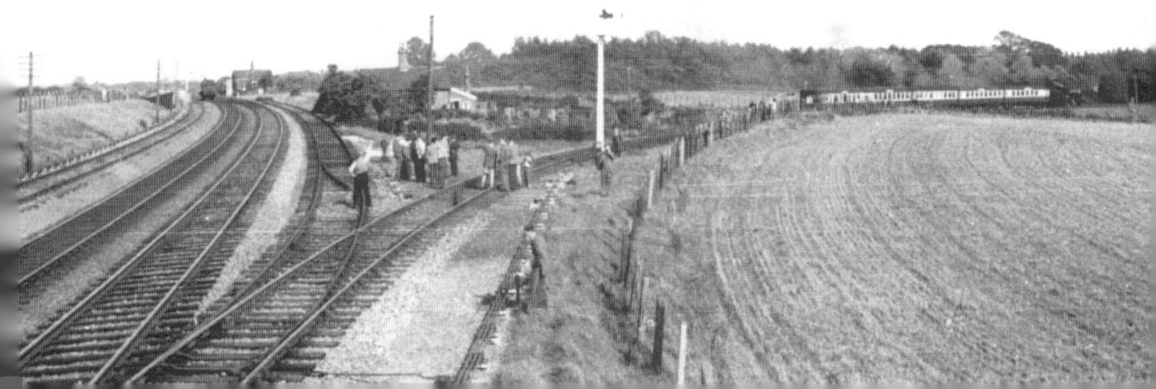

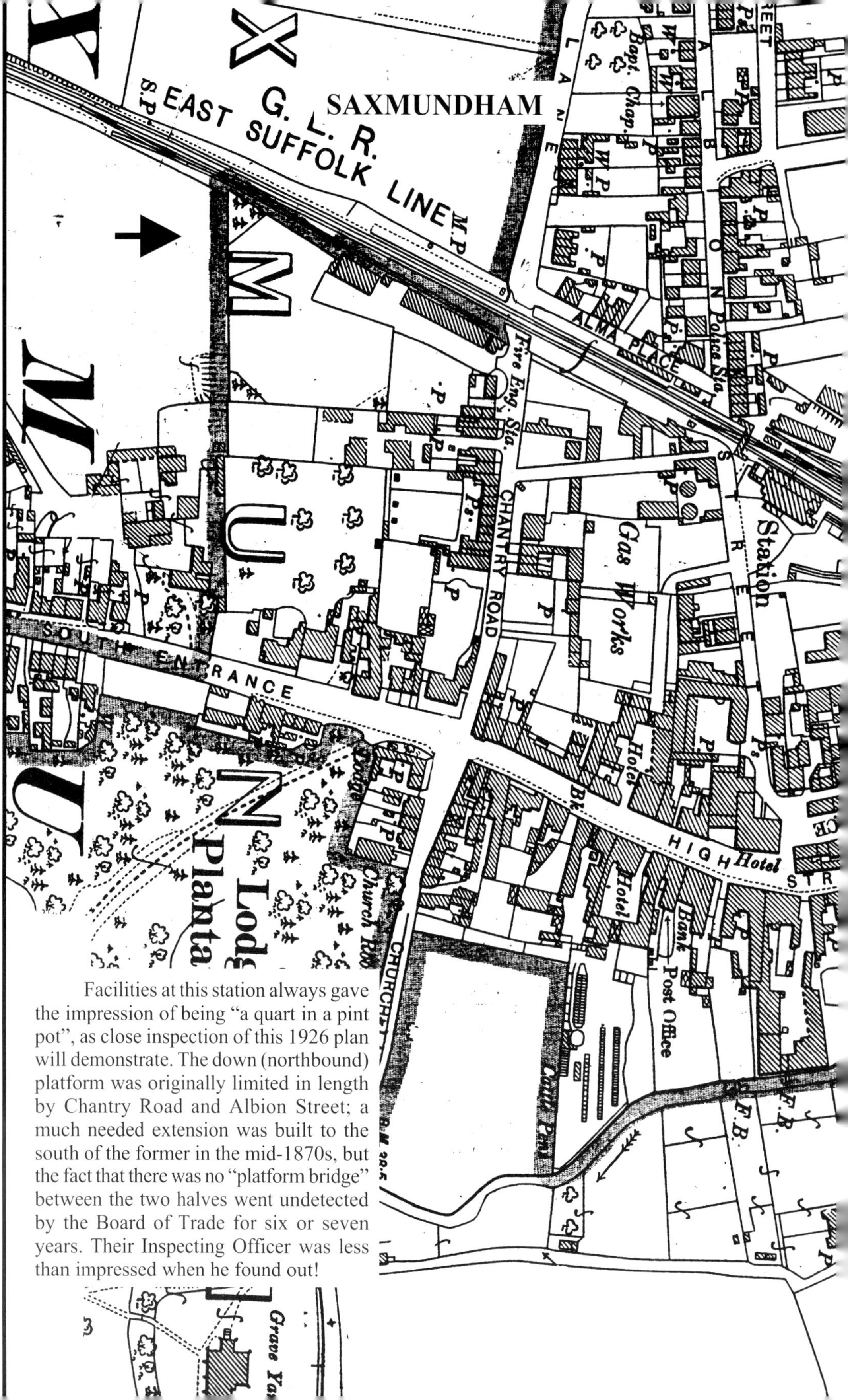

Facilities at this station always gave the impression of being "a quart in a pint pot", as close inspection of this 1926 plan will demonstrate. The down (northbound) platform was originally limited in length by Chantry Road and Albion Street; a much needed extension was built to the south of the former in the mid-1870s, but the fact that there was no "platform bridge" between the two halves went undetected by the Board of Trade for six or seven years. Their Inspecting Officer was less than impressed when he found out!

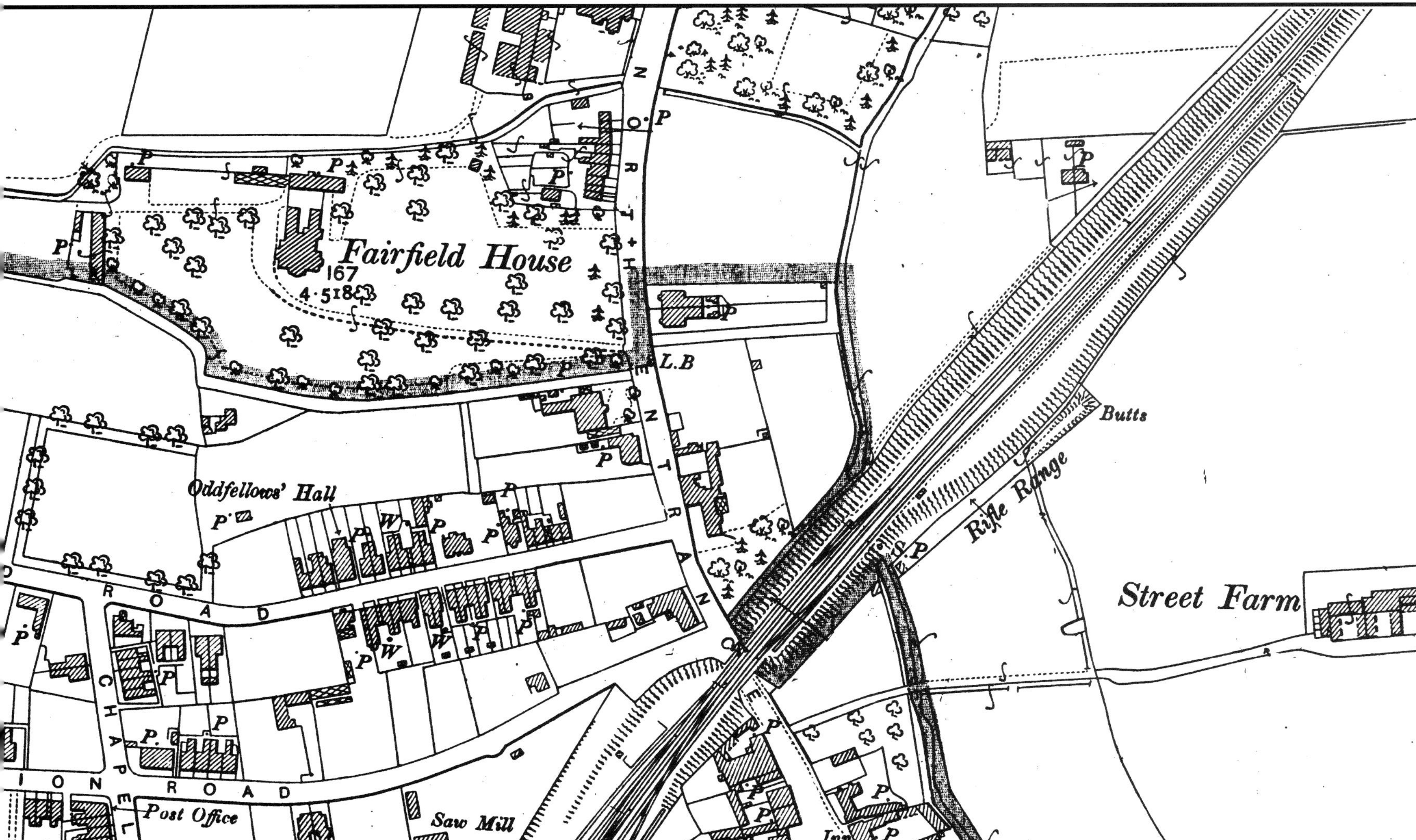
Fairfield House
167
4·518
NORTH
CENTRAL
Oddfellows' Hall
ROAD
CHAPEL
ION ROAD
Post Office
Saw Mill
L.B
Rifle Range
Butts
S.P
Street Farm
Inn

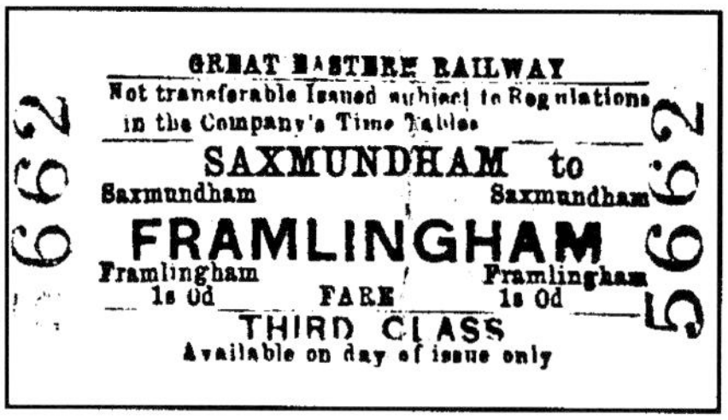

107. A boy peers at the photographer as he records the scene northwards over the level crossing in 1911. The number of rails in the level crossing would not have been welcomed by the local draymen as horses were prone to slip on such surfaces and then panic. Beyond the signal box, there is evidence of substantial goods traffic in the down yard. (HMRS)

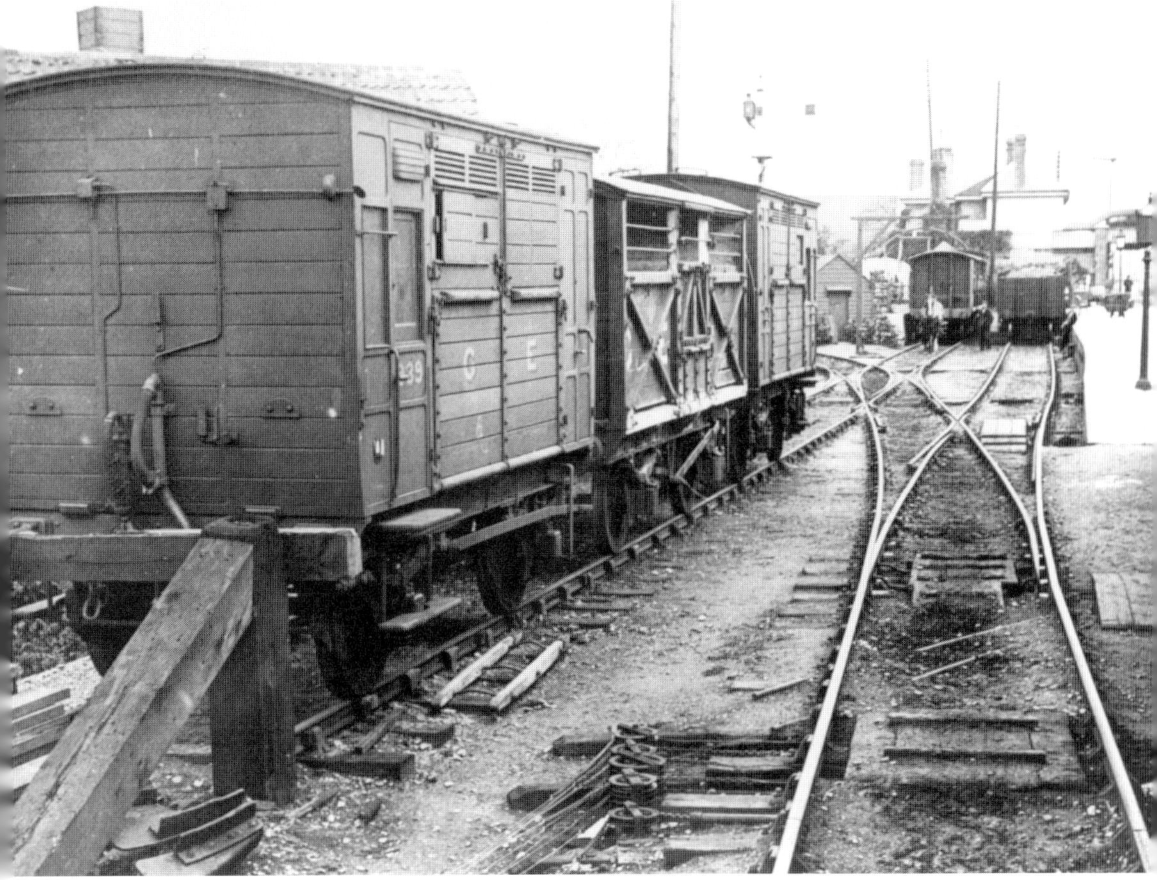

108. The somewhat cramped layout of the yard behind the up platform is evident in this 1911 picture. Two horse boxes and a cattle wagon occupy one siding, whilst beyond the loading gauge, a horse prepares to shunt another cattle wagon. (HMRS)

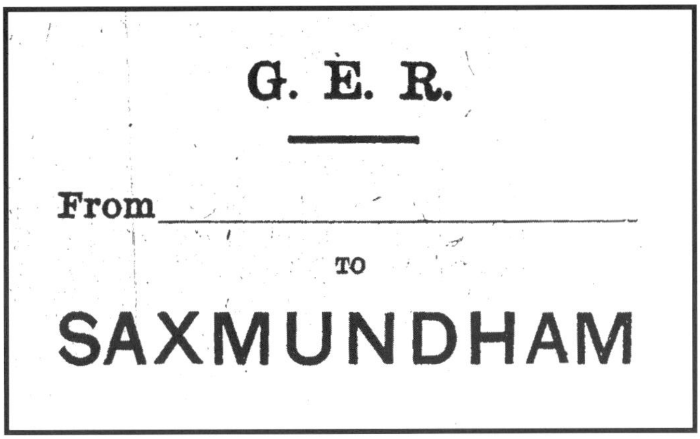
G. E. R.

From ______________________

TO

SAXMUNDHAM

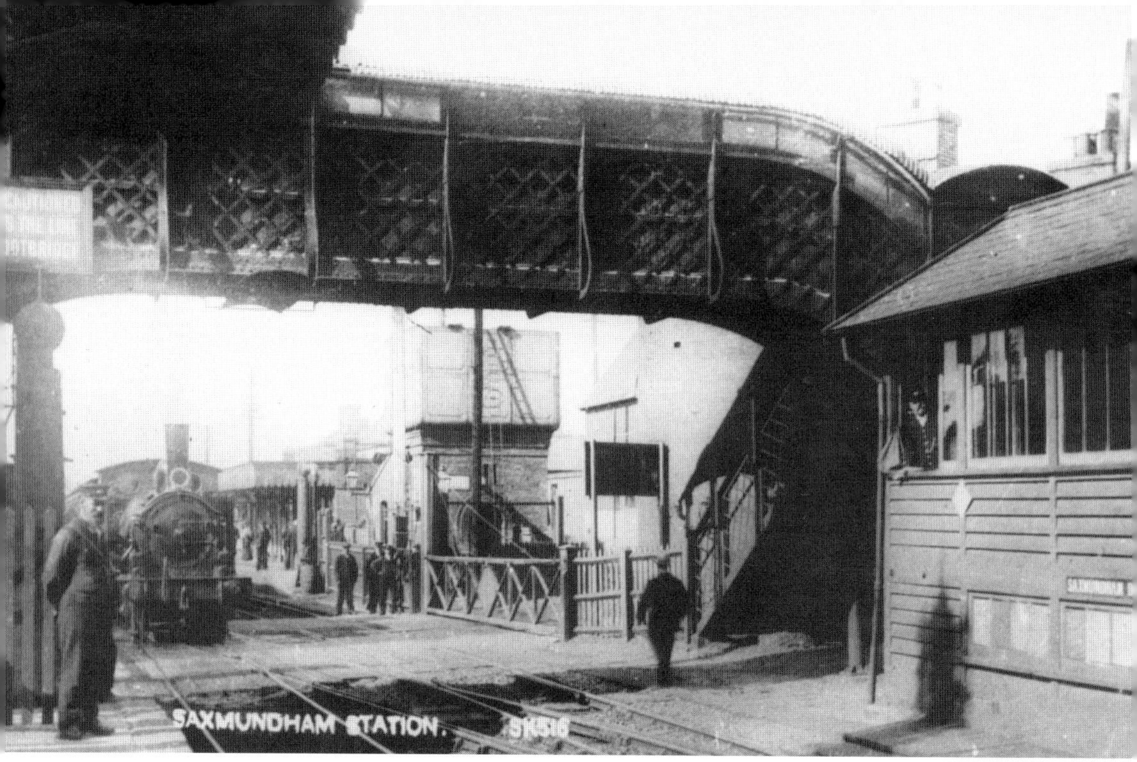

109. In the early days the footbridge boasted a corrugated iron roof to protect users from the elements. Looking south from the up platform around 1900, we see the down platform beyond the level crossing and water tower. (Lens of Sutton)

110. Some twenty years later, a fine collection of signs, advertising both the necessities and luxuries of life, brightened the somewhat dingy buildings on the down platform. (Stations UK)

111. Early in the motor age, road vehicles wait for passengers in the forecourt of the station. The weighing machine by the window is presumably sufficiently robust to survive exposure to the Suffolk weather! In the 1990s the buildings remained in use as a cafe and Tourist Information Centre. (Lens of Sutton)

112. A number of railwaymen pose beside class J15 0-6-0 no. 65388, which has been out on snowplough duty on a winters day in the 1950s. The wagon-mounted crane on the right merits more than a passing glance. (EADT)

113. Chantry Road cuts across the down platform, which was provided with a swinging section acting as a level crossing gate when a train was due. A member of the staff waits nonchalantly for a van to pass before closing the gap in the platform in August 1958. (Photomatic)

114. The level crossing has been swung across the road, thus creating a platform long enough for the main line trains. A small boy joins the station staff in wondering what a new Sulzer Type 2 diesel is doing with a passenger coach in the siding. (D.A.Jones)

115. The break in the platform is clearly shown in this view looking south from the footbridge some five years later, on 25th August 1965. Following an accident when an up train demolished the unopened swinging portion of the platform, conventional level crossing gates are now in place; however, the isolated southern section of the platform seems to be well maintained. (J.Watling)

116. A replacement down platform was built in the early 1980s on land formerly occupied by the goods yard. A class 105 DMU heads north from this new platform on 19th November 1982. Comparison with picture 107 will reveal many changes – and a surprising number of similarities. (H.N.James/J.Day)

SAXMUNDHAM

117. Despite what the destination blind says, this train is heading for Ipswich! The platform barrow, signal box, semaphore signal and ornate ironwork on the canopy all combine to create a traditional atmosphere as late as 10th April 1984. (R.J.Adderson)

118. Two three-car class 101 DMUs pause at the up platform on 23rd June 1984. At this time remodelling of the route was in progress, with single line working in force over the up line between here and Melton. This explains the token apparatus fouling the down line to the right of the picture. (D.C.Pearce)

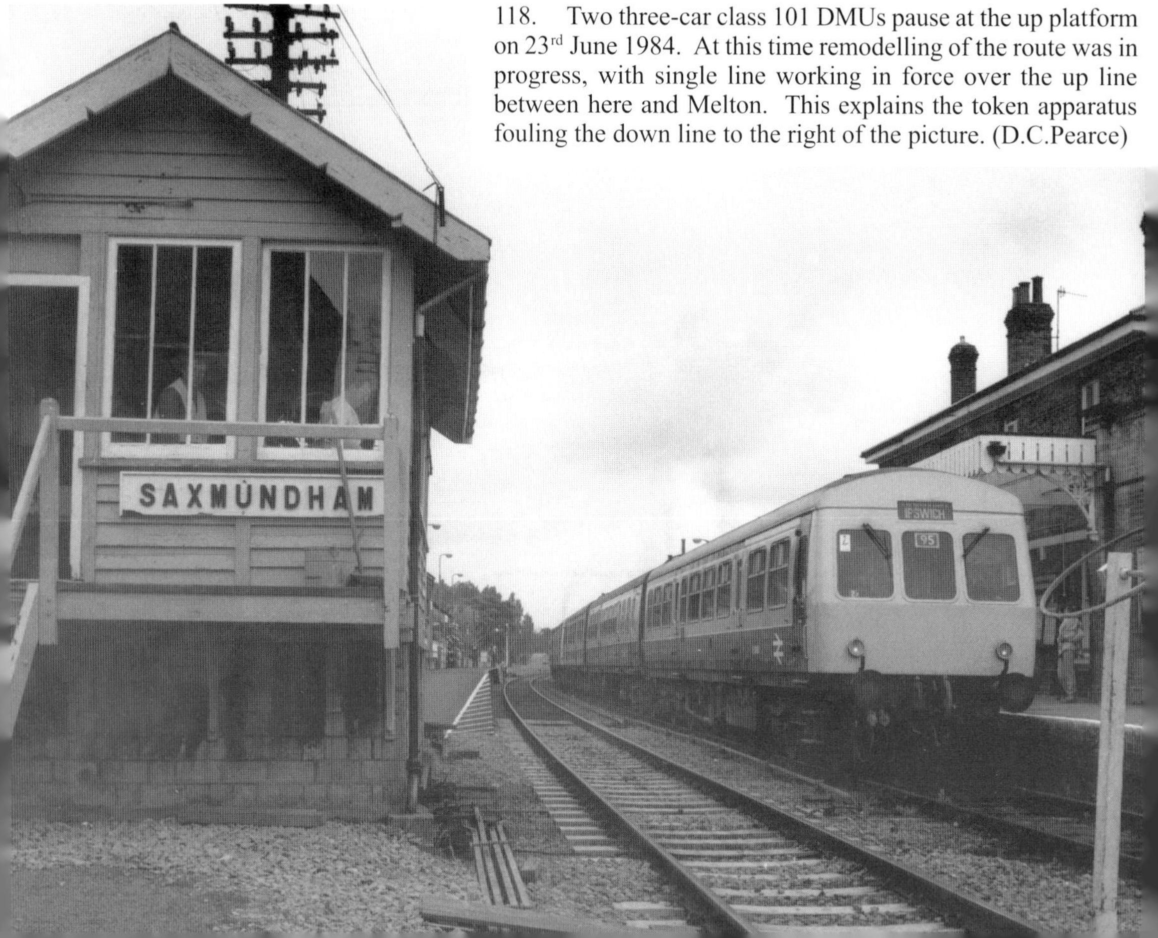

119. A class 153 rejoins the double track just south of the station in July 1999. The viewpoint for this photograph was close to the hut seen beyond the level crossing in picture 114, but nature has taken over to such an extent that only the distant bridge and the curvature of the track link the two pictures. Of the three locations on the line where there are single to double track points, those in this picture are the only ones which are not automatic, but are operated from the signal box so that trains bound for Sizewell can gain the up line through the station as far as Saxmundham Junction. (G.L.Kenworthy)

120. The signal box survived into the new era to act as the control centre for the radio signalling between Westerfield and Oulton Broad. It can just be seen on the left as passengers alight from no.153311 on 11th May 1999. (R.J.Adderson)

MP Middleton Press

Easebourne Lane, Midhurst, W Sussex. GU29 9AZ Tel: 01730 813169 Fax: 01730 812601
If books are not available from your local transport stockist, order direct with cheque, Visa or Mastercard, post free UK.

BRANCH LINES

Branch Line to Allhallows
Branch Line to Alton
Branch Lines around Ascot
Branch Line to Ashburton
Branch Lines around Bodmin
Branch Line to Bude
Branch Lines around Canterbury
Branch Lines around Chard & Yeovil
Branch Line to Cheddar
Branch Lines around Cromer
Branch Lines of East London
Branch Lines to Effingham Junction
Branch Lines around Exmouth
Branch Line to Fairford
Branch Lines around Gosport
Branch Line to Hawkhurst
Branch Line to Hayling
Branch Lines to Horsham
Branch Lines around Huntingdon
Branch Line to Kingswear
Branch Lines to Launceston & Princetown
Branch Lines to Longmoor
Branch Line to Looe
Branch Line to Lyme Regis
Branch Lines around March
Branch Lines around Midhurst
Branch Line to Minehead
Branch Line to Moretonhampstead
Branch Lines to Newport (IOW)
Branch Line to Padstow
Branch Lines around Plymouth
Branch Lines to Seaton and Sidmouth
Branch Line to Selsey
Branch Lines around Sheerness
Branch Line to Shrewsbury
Branch Line to Swanage *updated*
Branch Line to Tenterden
Branch Lines to Torrington
Branch Lines to Tunbridge Wells
Branch Line to Upwell
Branch Lines around Weymouth
Branch Lines around Wimborne
Branch Lines around Wisbech

NARROW GAUGE BRANCH LINES

Branch Line to Lynton
Branch Lines around Portmadoc 1923-46
Branch Lines around Porthmadog 1954-94
Two-Foot Gauge Survivors
Romneyrail

SOUTH COAST RAILWAYS

Ashford to Dover
Bournemouth to Weymouth
Brighton to Eastbourne
Chichester to Portsmouth
Dover to Ramsgate
Eastbourne to Hastings
Hastings to Ashford
Portsmouth to Southampton
Southampton to Bournemouth
Worthing to Chichester

SOUTHERN MAIN LINES

Basingstoke to Salisbury
Bromley South to Rochester
Charing Cross to Orpington
Crawley to Littlehampton
Dartford to Sittingbourne
East Croydon to Three Bridges
Epsom to Horsham
Exeter to Barnstaple
Exeter to Tavistock
Faversham to Dover
London Bridge to East Croydon
Orpington to Tonbridge
Tonbridge to Hastings
Salisbury to Yeovil
Swanley to Ashford
Tavistock to Plymouth
Victoria to East Croydon
Waterloo to Windsor
Waterloo to Woking
Woking to Portsmouth
Woking to Southampton
Yeovil to Exeter

EASTERN MAIN LINES

Fenchurch Street to Barking
Ipswich to Saxmundham
Liverpool Street to Ilford

WESTERN MAIN LINES

Paddington to Ealing

COUNTRY RAILWAY ROUTES

Andover to Southampton
Bath to Bristol
Bath to Evercreech Junction
Bournemouth to Evercreech Jn.
Croydon to East Grinstead
Didcot to Winchester
East Kent Light Railway
Fareham to Salisbury
Frome to Bristol
Guildford to Redhill
Porthmadog to Blaenau
Reading to Basingstoke
Reading to Guildford
Redhill to Ashford
Salisbury to Westbury
Stratford upon Avon to Cheltenham
Strood to Paddock Wood
Taunton to Barnstaple
Wenford Bridge to Fowey
Westbury to Bath
Woking to Alton
Yeovil to Dorchester

GREAT RAILWAY ERAS

Ashford from Steam to Eurostar
Clapham Junction 50 years of change
Festiniog in the Fifties
Festiniog in the Sixties
Isle of Wight Lines 50 years of change
Railways to Victory 1944-46
SECR Centenary album
Talyllyn 50 years of change
Yeovil 50 years of change

LONDON SUBURBAN RAILWAYS

Caterham and Tattenham Corner
Charing Cross to Dartford
Clapham Jn. to Beckenham Jn.
East London Line
Finsbury Park to Alexandra Palace
Kingston and Hounslow Loops
Lewisham to Dartford
Lines around Wimbledon
London Bridge to Addiscombe
Mitcham Junction Lines
North London Line
South London Line
West Croydon to Epsom
West London Line
Willesden Junction to Richmond
Wimbledon to Epsom

STEAMING THROUGH

Steaming through Cornwall
Steaming through Kent
Steaming through West Hants
Steaming through West Sussex

TRAMWAY CLASSICS

Aldgate & Stepney Tramways
Barnet & Finchley Tramways
Bath Tramways
Bournemouth & Poole Tramways
Brighton's Tramways
Camberwell & W.Norwood Tramwa
Clapham & Streatham Tramways
Dover's Tramways
East Ham & West Ham Tramways
Edgware and Willesden Tramways
Eltham & Woolwich Tramways
Embankment & Waterloo Tramways
Enfield & Wood Green Tramways
Exeter & Taunton Tramways
Gosport & Horndean Tramways
Greenwich & Dartford Tramways
Hammersmith & Hounslow Tramwa
Hampstead & Highgate Tramways
Hastings Tramways
Holborn & Finsbury Tramways
Ilford & Barking Tramways
Kingston & Wimbledon Tramways
Lewisham & Catford Tramways
Liverpool Tramways 1. Eastern Routes
Liverpool Tramways 2. Southern Routes
Maidstone & Chatham Tramways
North Kent Tramways
Portsmouth's Tramways
Reading Tramways
Seaton & Eastbourne Tramways
Shepherds Bush & Uxbridge Tramw
Southampton Tramways
Southend-on-sea Tramways
Southwark & Deptford Tramways
Stamford Hill Tramways
Thanet's Tramways
Twickenham & Kingston Tramways
Victoria & Lambeth Tramways
Waltham Cross & Edmonton Tramw
Walthamstow & Leyton Tramways
Wandsworth & Battersea Tramways

TROLLEYBUS CLASSICS

Croydon Trolleybuses
Bournemouth Trolleybuses
Hastings Trolleybuses
Maidstone Trolleybuses
Reading Trolleybuses
Woolwich & Dartford Trolleybuses

WATERWAY ALBUMS

Kent and East Sussex Waterways
London to Portsmouth Waterway
West Sussex Waterways

MILITARY BOOKS and VID

Battle over Portsmouth
Battle over Sussex 1940
Blitz over Sussex 1941-42
Bombers over Sussex 1943-45
Bognor at War
Military Defence of West Sussex
Secret Sussex Resistance
Sussex Home Guard
War on the Line
War on the Line VIDEO

OTHER BOOKS

Changing Midhurst
East Grinstead Then & Now
Garraway Father & Son
Index to all Stations
South Eastern & Chatham Railways
London Chatham & Dover Railway